W9-BCJ-569

The Elite Schools

The Elite Schools

A Profile of Prestigious
Independent Schools

Leonard L. Baird
Educational Testing Service

Lexington Books
D.C. Heath and Company
Lexington, Massachusetts
Toronto

For the right to reprint the copyrighted material quoted in this book, the author is indebted to the following publishers and authors:

Educational Testing Service and the Secondary School Research Program: For permission to use materials from *Questionnaire for Students, Teachers and Administrators* and *Questionnaire for New Students* (QUESTA I and QUESTA II), Preliminary Versions. Copyright © 1971, 1972 by Educational Testing Service. Reprinted by permission of Educational Testing Service and the Secondary School Research Program.

Educational Testing Service for permission to quote from *Independent Secondary Schools: A Handbook*, (First Edition, and Third Edition) Princeton, N.J.: Educational Testing Service (1971 and 1975).

The Johns Hopkins University Press for permission to quote from: Otto K. Kraushaar, *American Nonpublic Schools: Patterns of Diversity*. Baltimore: The Johns Hopkins University Press, © 1972.

Jossey-Bass, Inc. Publishers for permission to quote from: Kenneth A. Feldman and Theodore M. Newcomb, *The Impact of College on Students*. San Francisco: Jossey-Bass, 1969.

The National Association of Independent Schools for permission to quote from: Alan R. Blackmer, *An Inquiry into Student Unrest in Independent Schools*, Boston: National Association of Independent Schools, 1970.

Random House, Inc. for permission to quote from: Rolf E. Muuss, *Theories of Adolescence*, New York: Random House, Inc., © 1966.

Simon & Schuster, Inc. for permission to quote from: Richard L. Gaines, *The Finest Education Money Can Buy*, New York: Simon & Schuster, Inc., 1972. Copyright © 1972 by Richard L. Gaines.

Library of Congress Cataloging in Publication Data

Baird, Leonard.
    The elite schools.

    Bibliography: p.
    Includes index.
    1. Private schools—United States. I. Title.
LC49.B25   371'.02'0973   76-48376
ISBN 0-669-01146-0

International Standard Book Number: 0-669-01146-0

Library of Congress Catalog Card Number: 76-48376

To Rosanne

Contents

List of Tables

x

Acknowledgments

Many people were involved in this book. The thousands of students, teachers, and administrators who cooperated in the study, and were willing to share their opinions about their schools, must be thanked first. They reported their perceptions of the schools with exceptional articulateness and honesty. Obviously, without their help, this book would not have been possible. The schools which agreed to participate in the project deserve high praise for their willingness to have their internal workings opened to the study.

None of this would have been at all possible without the efforts of the Secondary School Research Program (SSRP), which encouraged the original project and supported the development of the basic instrument of the study and granted permission to quote from the instrument. Frederick Peterson of Phillips Academy, Andover, deserves special thanks for his role as the founder of SSRP, his energy and devotion in promoting its development, and his knowledge of the independent school world. Edward Dalton and Sanford Roeser of Educational Testing Service provided help in many invaluable ways. Educational Testing Service is to be thanked for its secretarial help, and its permission to quote from the instruments. Marian Helms, who typed almost all the manuscript (several times, during its various versions) and who handled much of the correspondence, form preparation, etc., during the course of the project, deserves thanks not only for her work, but for her cheerfulness and patience, especially when so many others, including myself, were sometimes sour and impatient.

Finally, I would like to express my enjoyment and exhilaration in conducting this study. The independent school students, teachers, and administrators I worked with were lively, alert, intelligent, and a delight to be with. I feel quite fortunate to have met and known so many people who have dedicated their lives to independent education—and who carried their dedication so happily.

Introduction

The elite independent schools have long played a unique and important role in American life. In the early years of the country, some of the schools were almost the only ones available for education for college. In more recent times, they have provided some of the best academic preparation for higher education. Even their nickname—"prep schools"—indicates how basic this function has been to the schools. They may voice other concerns, but they publicly and strongly endorse the purpose of helping their students gain the knowledge and skills necessary to get into and survive in college, particularly the most selective ones. Their catalogues often include impressive listings of the colleges their graduates have attended.

Historically, then, the independent schools have been elitist, in the sense of focusing on the preparation of students for the rigors of the college classroom. But the independent schools have also been—or at least have been accused of being—elitist because they train students from socially and financially select families. According to such critics as C. Wright Mills (1959) and Dornhoff (1967), these students later take over their parents' money, power, and positions in the banks, corporations, and political organizations that rule America. There is no question but that the schools number many distinguished and powerful people among their alumni. Statistical studies, similar to those of Mills and Dornhoff, have shown that many of the "power elite" of the corporate and financial world attended one of the selective independent schools, and other studies have shown that many important political leaders attended prep schools. Among many of the aristocratic families of America, attending one of the elite schools is a fourth or fifth generation tradition. But to show that wealthy and powerful families have sent their children to these schools is not to show that the schools' purpose is to help an elite perpetuate itself. Many teachers and administrators wish, along with Auchincloss' *Rector of Justin* (1965), that more of their graduates were "unsuccessful," because they were involved in low paying jobs such as teaching, social work in the slums, or sculpting. More to the point, as we shall see in the next chapter, only a small minority of the students who attend the elite schools come from families which could be called "elite." Furthermore, we shall see later that many of the students would be surprised to be considered among the children of the powerful.

Although it is clear that the independent schools have educated generations of students who then entered the social, as well as intellectual, elites of our society, the schools are, in fact, most concerned with, and most proud of, their provision of high quality educations for their students. Academic excellence is the very heart of their purpose and life. However, in their concentration on their academic and philosophical goals the elite schools create very intense social and educational environments. They have been described as academic pressure cookers—forcing their students to study more and more about smaller and smaller subjects. The very words so favored by elite-school educators—challenge, enrichment, acceleration—imply demands for performances beyond what would "naturally" be expected. This pressure for *academic* excellence sometimes interferes with intellectual or personal excellence. As one student in a school outside Boston told me, "I would love to go into the city to see a play or attend a concert or go to the museums or just walk around Harvard Square, but I have so much homework to do that I never have the time."

The pressures of the environment are most intense in the boarding schools. The students study, eat, sleep, exercise, talk, and play at the school. Students' daily activities are scheduled from the morning alarm to the last light at night. Even the "free" time is, in reality, structured. The formal activities a student can "freely" engage in are prescribed and approved by the school. Many students also have to use their free time to study to keep up with the academic work. In these circumstances, the most benign school can sometimes seem like a prison to students. The schools exert overt and subtle pressures on their students every moment. Thus, the elite schools are not just classrooms and books—they are total environments organized to reach certain goals. For many of their students the total environment of the prep school is the most intense and all encompassing experience of their lives except for their early childhood years with their families. In fact, most of the schools are organized to serve many of the functions of the family as well as an educational institution, and the schools pride themselves on their intimate concern for the student. In the house system used at many schools, a faculty family lives in the same house with the students.

The elite schools, then, are extremely unusual social environments in the American experience. It is hard to imagine a stronger effort by American educators to influence students than is found in the independent schools. It thus becomes a matter of general interest to discover whether the independent school system is effective and to learn how it operates. It may be very useful to other schools to learn about the culture of the elite schools, to provide lessons, if not to provide a model they could follow.

The independent schools have also sometimes served as laboratories for new educational ideas. Although some schools are proud of staying the same in every respect, many have experimented with programs of community service in hospitals, ghetto schools, and homes for the elderly or crippled. Some have tried new approaches in the classroom. Some have experimented with the curriculum. Some have changed and simplified the grading system. Some have involved students in the governance of the school. Not all these programs have worked, and few have been fundamental, but they take place in a context that makes the evaluation of their consequences and costs easier than in the public schools. Not only can the rest of the students' experiences be taken into consideration, but the *unintended* consequences are more apparent to the school because of the intimacy of school life.

Many of the experiments, as Blackmer (1970) has well described, are school responses to changes in the society since, in many ways, the schools are microcosms of the changing larger society. As in the rest of American life, the traditional values of the schools have been challenged; the values of striving for success, working hard for the sake of working hard, competing, and adhering to the expectations of one's family and religion have been questioned, if not openly derided. Many schools faced with the problem of filling openings, must recruit a different kind of student than the students they attracted in the past. The teachers in some schools feel that their recent students, if not less able, are less academically inclined and more rebellious and resentful of authority. In addition, some schools have deliberately recruited students from backgrounds that may not be conducive to educational attainment. Like many other modern organizations, the schools also face financial problems. Increased operating expenses, difficulties in retaining students, and faculty demands for higher salaries all increase the pressures on the schools to retrench, cut costs, eliminate programs, curtail activities, and avoid expensive innovations.

In sum, these various challenges to the schools—the questioning of values, the new kinds of students, the financial pressure—add to the schools' difficulties in meeting a more fundamental challenge: criticism of the basic social role of the schools. Many people now believe that we do not need such schools, or feel that they are undemocratic, or think that the schools serve to perpetuate an outmoded class system. The schools' emphasis on academic skills and knowledge seems to many of their students to be too narrow, one-sided, and archaic. Many students reject the track of secondary school to college to career or more education, and feel the schools should train students "for life not just for college," as one student put it.

Independent schools have played an important role in American life for many years. They have schooled many in the social and intellectual elites of our society. For that reason alone they would deserve study. But they are also intense social and educational environments concentrating on specific moral and academic goals. They have sometimes been laboratories of education. And finally, they are microcosms of the changes in the society—their traditional values have been criticized, new methods have been introduced, new kinds of students are attending, the schools face financial pressures, and most important, the basic social role of the schools has been challenged. Independent schools seem to deserve intensive study.

The pages that follow will describe the life of these schools as it is experienced by their students, teachers, and administrators. The next chapter describes the history and characteristics of the schools. The following chapter is devoted to a description of the students, the reasons they and their parents choose independent schools, and their hopes and fears for their years in independent schools. The friendships, social groups, and sources of status among students are also examined in this chapter. The sensitive and changing role of minority students in the schools will be considered next. In the following chapter, the lives of teachers, their behavior in and out of class, and their critical role in the schools will be discussed. We will then examine the formal structure of the schools as reflected in three questions: who runs the schools? how well do the people in the school communicate with each other? and, which actions are permissible, and which are not? The important area of the nonacademic program is also examined. The discussion then turns to the core of the schools: the values of the students, teachers, and administrators, and the purposes and goals of the schools. This leads directly to a consideration of the consequences of the schools, both in their pressures on students and their influence on students' values and aspirations. Finally, we will try to assess the value of an elite school education, and ponder the future of the schools.

The basis for this discussion is information gathered from some 3,400 third- and fourth-year students and 1,000 teachers and administrators in forty-two independent schools, most in the northeast. All of these people completed an extensive questionnaire about their schools. In addition, information about the expectations, hopes, and fears of students who enter these schools for the first time was gathered from a survey of 4,600 new students in the schools. (More detail about these surveys may be found in Appendix A.) The survey responses were supplemented and illuminated by several thousand comments written by students, teachers, and administrators, and many face-to-face interviews. Wherever possible, the views of students, teachers, and administrators are compared and contrasted to gain an understanding of the schools' human dynamics.

This book is a report on an intensive study of the schools—their students, teachers and administrators and their social and educational environments. This book represents an attempt to understand the *culture* of the elite independent schools.

The Elite Schools

1

The Schools—Different but the Same

The forty-two independent schools in this study tend to look much the same on the outside.[a] The well-kept lawns, stately buildings, and students with armfuls of books rushing to class present the same picture of calm peace at most schools. The students in the various schools seem to have fairly similar backgrounds. The teaching in the small classes looks about the same from school to school. Although the schools share these and many other characteristics, appearances can be deceiving. The schools differ in many ways.

First, let's look at their age. Although nearly all are old, some are much older than others. Only six of the schools were founded after World War I, and only fourteen were founded after the turn of the century; eleven are nearly a century old. The remaining seventeen schools are at least one hundred years old and five of those were founded before 1800. The fact of age is not very important as a physical fact. There are new buildings and equipment on nearly all campuses, and the old ones are well maintained. However, age is important as a psychological fact. The schools have histories, stories, and traditions that influence the behavior of students and teachers alike. There is a feeling that the past is important, and that precedents add authority to rules and procedures. (McLachlan (1970) has provided a fine history of the development of boarding schools which illustrates the importance of the past.)

Similarly, the relatively small enrollments of the schools (from less than 200 to more than 900) are not particularly important as a statistical fact. Rather, it is the intimacy of the schools' interpersonal climate that the schools' small sizes make possible that is important. It is still possible, but unlikely, that a student can become one of the socially invisible "nonpersons" that often pass through large public schools in such small schools. The intensity of the small elite school environment also has costs, of course, as we shall see throughout this book. Whatever its drawbacks, education in a small school is very different than education in a large school. For example, Cushing Academy students stage nearly a dozen plays a year. They report that over half the students participate in these plays in some capacity—actors, stagehands, or set builders. The small size of the schools means that a high proportion of the student body participates in school activities.

Four of the schools have a formal commitment to a particular religion and a

---

[a]The schools and the surveys of them are described in Appendix A. The sample does not include every one of the "best" independent schools, but it does include a good cross-section of the more prestigious schools. They are listed in Appendix B.

1

few more encourage religious observance, but most are truly nonsectarian. However, some "nonsectarian" schools are quite religious. For example, the Hill School lists itself as nonsectarian, but has required courses in theology and philosophy, taught by the schools' chaplain. In addition, there are a number of "Christian" courses in the curriculum.

One thing that may surprise many people is the high cost of the schools. Although there is some variation in the tuition and fees, they are all expensive. The typical cost of a day school is between $1,800 and $2,600 for an academic year, and the typical cost of a boarding school ranges between $3,300 and $4,500 for an academic year.[b] These figures do not include such expenses as books, laundry, special fees, travel, pocket money, or clothing. The costs for girls' schools average somewhat higher than the costs for boys' schools for two reasons; they have smaller endowments and less alumni support than boys' schools, and parents often expect more comforts and facilities for their daughters than for their sons. Although the costs are high, some schools are rather spartan, while some have lavish facilities. These high costs have powerful consequences for the kind of students that attend the schools. Only well-to-do families can send their children to the elite schools without sacrifice, and students from such families are the majority in the elite schools. However, a large number of families of moderate means do make the necessary sacrifices to send their children to the schools. They do so because they believe the quality of the educations their children receive is worth their scrimping and saving. The schools also have scholarship and loan programs to attract bright but poor students. Thus, like some selective colleges, the elite schools enroll the wealthy and able, the dedicated, and the poor and bright. (The social composition of the elite schools' student bodies is described in greater detail in the next chapter.)

The schools differ dramatically in a related area, the sizes of their endowments. These vary from a few thousand dollars to several million dollars. NAIS figures indicate that the average endowment for girls' boarding schools was about $1 million in 1969. For boys' boarding schools it was about $5 million. Nine of the schools in this study had endowments of $10 million or more. The figures have not changed dramatically since then because of the ups and downs of the stock market in subsequent years; most endowments are invested in stocks and bonds. (Kraushaar (1972) has provided detailed information about the size and meaning of the endowments of private schools.) The larger the endowment, the less the school must depend on tuition and fees, and the more able is the school to start innovative and experimental programs.

The curricula of the schools may be described as standard academic—English, mathematics, science, and languages—with some electives. (Undoubtedly, this unabashed devotion to academic subjects appeals to many parents who are tired of the nonintellectual courses offered in their local public schools.) The

[b]The schools point out that tuition and boarding fees only represent two-thirds to one-half of the costs to the schools. The rest of the cost is paid from endowments and gifts.

number and variety of the electives vary from school to school. In some schools the "electives" are really more of the same academic material. In others, the courses include "The Literature of Protest," "Japanese Literature," "Existential-ism and Modern Philosophy," "Utopias," and "The Relations of Women and Men in Modern Society." In some schools these courses are initiated by students who often feel that the traditional courses are too narrow and academic. However, part of the students' desire for a voice in the curriculum may be a desire to control their own lives. One English teacher told how students criticized a course in Shakespeare as an elective because it seemed too traditional and narrow. The students then organized their own program of electives, and one of the most popular courses they planned was a course in Shakespeare!

Several schools schedule a period between semesters during which students can participate in a wide variety of short courses and revitalize their enthusiasm for learning. For example, Ethel Walker's "Lacuna" provides some fifty mini courses, which have ranged from views on death and immortality to auto mechanics. Miss Porter's School has a "Winterim" of five weeks during which students have studied topics ranging from "Quilting" to "The Third Reich."

Some of the schools separate students of different levels of ability into different tracks or "streams." They distinguish between students who excel at mathematics or foreign languages and those who do not, in the belief that groups of students of similar talents can be taught more effectively. (This practice sometimes meets with scathing criticism in public schools.) The schools also demonstrate their impassioned devotion to the academic in their use of tests. For example, hour tests are held at least once a month in courses at Williston-Northampton and final examinations take place at the end of the fall, winter, and spring terms. Teachers' written comments about students' work are provided at least once a term. Since college placement is a basic task of the school, the College Board tests assume enormous importance. In many schools, courses explicitly or tacitly include preparation for the College Board tests as part of the coursework. For example, at Phillips Academy, Andover, various chemistry, mathematics, and history courses are frankly listed as providing preparation for the College Board tests in those areas. Unfortunately, this emphasis on college admission tests makes some students believe that the tests will determine the entire course of their lives, and this makes them very anxious.

The schools' schedules also show their academic orientation. Some of the schools schedule classes on Saturdays, and almost all of the schools include mandatory study periods for students, with the usual exception of twelfth graders. In some schools, such as the Avon Old Farms School, the amount of time students must spend in the study hall is directly related to their grades; the lower their grades, the longer the study period.

A few schools have struck out in new directions. For example, Walnut Hill has a school of performing arts which serves students who seek in-depth study of music, dance, theater, painting, sculpture, and photography. Wykeham Rise

School, a relatively new school, provides instruction in dance, drama, music, creative writing, photography, and studio arts at three levels: introductory, major, and pre-professional. Their list of graduate placements includes Julliard, the Joffrey Ballet School, the Neighborhood Playhouse, and the Boston Museum School, as well as Smith, Sarah Lawrence, and Yale. Cushing Academy has a strong natural science program that emphasizes field work and animal ecology. Some schools, such as the Lawrence Academy, provide "alternative curricula" in which students assume responsibility for their own education. Students and faculty work out a plan specifying the objectives, content, structure, and evaluation of the student's education. These programs allow the students great latitude in their work, so that they may follow their own interests, and develop their special talents. However, this flexibility does not mean that academic standards are let down; in some cases they are even higher than in the standard program. For example, at Lawrence Academy graduation is by vote of the faculty.

These schools illustrate a trend that makes a good deal of educational sense. Some schools have worked out unique and specialized programs which give them an important central focus. Rather than duplicating the programs of every other school, these schools have decided to capitalize on their special strengths and have sought students with special talent or interest in their areas of strength. This means that the students' educational experiences can be much better planned and coordinated, with a much stronger impact on students' development. In addition, many schools offer educational experiences which are seldom found in the ordinary public school, such as trips abroad in France, Spain, Germany, or Italy for students who are sufficiently advanced in the language of the country.

In general, the academic quality of the schools seems, to an external observer, to be most impressive. The classes are very small; most schools try to keep them no larger than twelve to fifteen students. The overall student-teacher ratios are low. The total variety of academic courses is great. Language instruction, for example, usually includes several languages, sometimes going beyond French, Spanish, and Latin to include Russian, Greek, Arabic, or Chinese, taught in language laboratories as well as classrooms. The facilities are usually first rate. Libraries typically have thousands of volumes, and some libraries surpass the average college in size and variety. For example, Andover's[c] library includes over 100,000 volumes, which is more than the library holdings at Bennington College. A number of campuses include art galleries, computers, radio and TV stations, golf courses, skating rinks, horse stables, and planetariums. Many independent schools have special programs to further enrich their students' academic and personal growth, such as Abbot's Washington Internship program, and the Northfield-Mt. Hermon school's term in France or Spain.

[c]Phillips Academy at Andover is universally referred to as "Andover" in the independent school world. It will be described as Andover throughout the rest of this book.

Finally, although, as we shall see, the schools draw most of their students from a fairly narrow part of the social class distribution, their student body is diverse in other ways. Many elite independent schools are national schools, drawing students from many areas. Andover, for example, has reported enrolling students from all states and thirty-six foreign countries, Emma Willard from thirty states and seventeen countries, and Deerfield from thirty-six states and twenty countries.

Most schools sit on fairly extensive parcels of land; the average is probably over one hundred acres, and some are quite large, such as the Kent School (1,523 acres in the boys' campus and 675 acres in the girls' campus) and Northfield-Mt. Hermon, with 4,400 acres. This land allows schools to provide "wilderness" experiences, hiking areas, nature-study areas, lakes for swimming, sailing, and skating, and private places for students to be alone. The fact that many of the schools are boarding schools means that they must provide many services for students which would ordinarily be provided by a community. For example, the schools must have at least a visiting physician, and most have infirmaries. Choate has a hospital with a physician, seven nurses, and a physiotherapist. In addition, the schools have stores, facilities for hobbies, etc. The extent of these educational facilities can be seen in the estimates of the worth of the physical plants of the schools. Most are worth several million dollars, and some, such as Choate, with a campus valued at $20 million and Northfield-Mt. Hermon with facilities valued at $39 million, represent sizable enterprises. (They may be even more sizable than these estimates suggest; most schools list their physical assets at purchase cost rather than current or replacement value.) The richness of the facilities does not mean that students live in luxury. In fact, most students' quarters are quite spartan, and, especially in the boarding schools, students must do some maintenance work or perform house duties. However, in general, the schools have taken care to provide for the physical needs of the students, and have gone to extraordinary efforts to provide first-rate facilities for learning. In sum, the elite schools seem to be very rich in academic and human resources.

The majority of the schools in the study are single-sex schools: twenty-three are boys' schools and nine are girls' schools; five others are coeducational schools and five are "coordinate" schools. Coordinate schools share some teachers and facilities but have separate schools for boys and girls, each with its own faculty and student body. The single-sex schools have a singular character. The tensions of sexual frustration add to the usual problems of school life. Many students feel confined in an unnatural environment. To some the lack of the opposite sex seems to increase the concern with sex rather than lessening it. As one student at a boys' school described it, "The possibility of a student to meet anyone of the opposite sex is nil. Every student that leaves on vacation is so keyed up and horny, I wouldn't doubt if some of them have raped." We shall return to the questions of sex and coeducation later in this book.

Most of the schools in the study (thirty-five) were boarding schools; seven were day schools. The boarding schools actually vary considerably in their rules and procedures, but overall, Kraushaar's (1972) account of their atmosphere seems reasonably descriptive:

It is the totality of the boarding situation which engenders the (students') sense of confinement and unreality. It is in part the restriction on freedom for senior students in maturity, or at least in sophistication, the equivalent of a college freshman or sophomore a generation ago: compulsory attendance in each of the schools' activities, rules and checkins which seem to the impatient ones the customs and conventions of another age. The frustration, in part, also comes from a sense of being overprotected, oversheltered from the stormy blast. The mature student is eager to widen his experience, to 'bust loose' and get where the action is.

Even the most benign boarding schools may seem oppressive because of the totality of the environment, even to the point of dampening students' desire for learning.

The character of boarding school life can be sensed in Groton's and Loomis-Chaffee's descriptions of their daily routines in the *Independent Secondary Schools: A Handbook.*

A normal day at Groton begins at 7 with breakfast, followed on four days a week by a short chapel service at 8, eight 40-minute classes, and cafeteria lunch from 12:20 to 1:20. The afternoon is devoted to athletics and other extracurricular activities followed by supper at 6:15. Meals are well attended by faculty and families. The evenings are devoted to studies with the eighth graders in study halls and the older students in their own rooms. Committee meetings, athletic contests, visits to faculty homes, and trips to the town of Groton are a few of the other activities possible during the day.

It takes energy to get through a day at Loomis-Chaffee. Breakfast is at 7:15 and day students arrive for assembly at 8:10. Classes begin at 8:35 and end at 3:15 with time out for lunch and an activities period. Since classes are held every other Saturday, the school operates on an 11-day cycle and each day's schedule is different. Sports are from 3:30 until after 5. There are no classes or intramural practices on Wednesday or Saturday afternoons when varsity and j.v. games are played. Day students normally go home after sports but sometimes stay for supper at 6:15 in order to attend rehearsals or other activities before study hall at 7:30. Freshmen and sophomores are expected to be in bed by 10:30. Juniors and seniors determine their own "late lights." Faculty and students alike take part in the work program which involves several hours each week. Work jobs are built into each individual's schedule and involve working in the dining hall, cleaning buildings, or taking care of the grounds.

As these quotes suggest, one feature of boarding school life is that nearly every moment in a student's life is planned and scheduled. At almost any time of the day, a student can be "accounted for"; the implication being that students *must* be accounted for. The assumption is that students can only be trusted with minor decisions; major decisions should be made for them. Many students feel that the choices available to them have been carefully selected by others who presume to know what is best for them. Many feel no real freedom to be themselves. Many feel encapsulated in a closed social system where they have no say about their own lives. For example, consider the view of some students about their schools:

I think it is very unfortunate that the students in this school are encumbered by the restrictions made out of a idealistic concept of the All-American boy. There are no outlets for expression other than classroom discussions, for everything else is censored or destroyed.

There are no forms of art, music, or any creative courses available at this institution. Even political and racial views are limited and strongly influenced. There is no inspiration for work, for there are no rewards. One is truly on ones own initiative and surface ability.

If there was a greater understanding of the personal feelings of the individuals, possibly there would be hope for an opening of many new areas for great opportunity. I find myself with my hands tied.

The students feel that they are being treated as dependent children far beyond the age when they feel ready to control, at least partially, their own lives. The number of rules, the restrictions, the pettiness of enforcement are all probably not much greater than those they faced at home. But in the schools the rules are institutionalized rather than personalized. To these students personal arbitrariness may seem more understandable and less odious than institutional arbitrariness. And, students can usually appeal a decision or rule to their parents at the dinner table, but there are usually no such options in the independent schools short of formal appeals or mass movements.

Another characteristic which makes the elite schools unique and which adds to the feelings just described, is their location. Nearly half, nineteen, are in the rural countryside, fifteen others are located in small towns; only eight are in urban settings, and only one of these is in a major city. The location of the schools suggests that most are isolated, or at least not surrounded by the problems of the cities or suburbs. (The Hebron Academy is six miles from the next closest rural Maine town, and sixteen miles from the second closest.) This isolation almost certainly adds to students' feelings that they are completely subject to the rules and procedures of the schools with few options for life outside the schools. Finally, all but five of the study schools were in the East; seven were in the middle Atlantic states, and thirty were in New England. The traditions of this area very probably help to form part of the unique culture of the elite schools, provide fewer openings for students who would wish to change the schools, and contribute to an increased sense of isolation. In areas where the schools have been a tradition for a century or more, there may be little outside encouragement of criticisms of the ways things have been.

In sum, the schools in this study, like many independent schools, differ among themselves, but share many characteristics that make their environments unique and intense. Most of them are old single-sex boarding schools in the country or small towns, located in the Northeast. Altogether these factual characteristics of the schools combine to produce environments with an intensity and all-encompassing quality that produces the positive and the deleterious effects which we will examine in the following chapters.

2

The Students: What They Bring to the Schools

The best place to begin an examination of the elite schools is with the incoming students. Every teacher knows that the characteristics of a class—whether the students are bright or dull, disruptive or serious, alert or careless—can make or break a school year. If it is a "good" class, students will make a lot of progress; if it is not, students may learn very little. The same logic applies to schools. If schools traditionally draw students who dislike school work, who are sullen, and who are prone to violence, then the schools' graduates will very probably look bad, even if the schools have well designed and well conducted programs. On the other hand, if schools traditionally draw students who are bright, academically inclined, cheerful, and cooperative, then their graduates will probably look good, even if the schools have programs which are poorly designed and ineptly conducted. The quality of the students who enter a school obviously has a lot to do with the quality of the students who graduate. The school which gets good students will have good graduates and may mistakenly assume it is doing an effective job.

It is also easy for schools to assume that they are doing a good job because their students are obviously brighter and more mature as twelfth graders than they were when they entered the school. However, these changes may be largely due to the maturation of the students. Seventeen and eighteen year olds are much more mature than thirteen and fourteen year olds. A fair assessment of the schools' effectiveness requires a clear understanding of the quality and characteristics of the entering students, so that this information can be a benchmark against which one may assess the progress of students.

What kind of students attend the elite schools? The students who responded to the survey of entering students are not a typical cross-section of American students. The schools include many of the finest schools in America, and the students tend to reflect the unusual quality of the schools.[a] First, they are well off. The average income of the families of elite school students was about $40,000 in 1976. (National figures indicated that only about 2 percent of families made $40,000 or more.) Their parents were also well educated; 80 percent of the fathers and 60 percent of the mothers had a bachelor's degree or more. Before these figures are dismissed as the exaggerations of students, it should be noted that Kraushaar's (1972) figures for family income, taken from the parents themselves, were nearly identical to those provided by students. The

[a]The survey which is the basis for these descriptions is described in Appendix A under the *Questionnaire for New Students*.

9

students in these schools clearly came from unusually high social and educational backgrounds. Furthermore, nearly all were white. Only about 6 percent were minority students, although nearly 10 percent were from minority families in boys' boarding schools.

Most elite school students are not from "power elite" families, but most are clearly from upper middle class and upper class homes. It seems probable that few of the students have felt any of the family financial pressures that are so common in our society, and few have felt any serious degree of deprivation. Very few poor or working class students go to the elite schools, in spite of scholarship and aid programs. Many of the children of high level corporate and governmental executives do attend the elite schools, although they form a minority of the student body. However, it is easy to exaggerate the effect of the students' high status on the schools. The children themselves are often unaware of the power or positions of their parents or relatives. In one girls' school, for example, the girls wrote angry letters of protest to the companies they believed were polluting the local rivers. Many girls were startled to get back letters that began "Dear Sue," or "Dear Jane," from their uncles, cousins, grandfathers, or neighbors who were vice presidents or comptrollers for the companies.

The students enter independent schools with extremely high ambitions; virtually all of the students said they would definitely or probably go to college. The students also overwhelmingly planned to graduate from college (88 percent overall) and the majority planned some degree requiring work beyond the bachelor's (about 55 percent). Thus, as a group, these students seem to be highly motivated to achieve advanced degrees. Of course, in this mobile and technological society, most children from well-educated families might be expected to aspire to degrees that will at least allow them to retain their present status.

Selection for the Elite Schools

Analogous to the admissions to selective colleges, there are admissions barriers besides the economic and social barriers to attendance at independent schools. Many elite schools are as selective as the most exclusive colleges. For example, Groton and Exeter have five or six "final" applicants for every new student enrolled, and Choate-Rosemary Hall advises parents to file an application a year in advance. The elite schools carefully examine the previous academic records of students who apply for admission. The applicants usually must have taken the Secondary School Admission Test, which is similar to the Scholastic Aptitude Test used to assess the strengths of applicants to colleges. Almost all the schools require an interview, and many require recommendations from teachers and principals at previous schools. (Peter Prescott, in his book on Choate (1970), describes a typical interview between an applicant and the Choate admission officer. The interview ranged from discussions of the student's reasons for applying to Choate, to the student's recent reading and vocabulary.) A number of schools also ask for other data they have found useful in assessing students, including intelligence test scores, writing assignments, and estimates of the applicant's "enthusiasm" for college preparatory work. This information is usually examined by an admission committee of teachers and administrators, which discusses each applicant's qualifications, and recommends acceptance or rejection.

The result of this selection is that the students are unusually bright and highly motivated. Their previous academic records are good. Their intelligence test results, their Secondary School Admissions Test scores, and their later College Board scores all provide evidence that the elite school students are quite able. In fact, it is probably rare to find a student with an intelligence quotient below 100, the hypothetical average, in an elite school classroom, and it is not uncommon to find several students with intelligence quotients above 140, termed "gifted" by some experts. Figures summarized by the Educational Records Bureau indicate that the *average* independent school student scores above the ninetieth percentile of all secondary school students on tests of academic ability and achievement. Some of the students also have high level abilities in other areas, such as music, language, and science. As we have just seen, the students were also already planning college and graduate and professional school careers which match their abilities.

A Digression on the College Placement of Elite School Graduates

Of course, the high expectations of elite school students are only to be expected, since the student's aspirations reflect their parents' hopes. One of the basic assumptions made by many parents, who pay thousands of dollars to send their children to the independent schools, is that their children's chances for entrance to highly selective colleges will be much greater if they apply from an independent school than if they apply from a public school. Although the schools try to reduce the unrealistic expectations of parents, many, if not most of the parents believe that their child should get into one of the "best" colleges. The truth is that only the very best students will be able to attend Harvard, Stanford, Yale, Princeton, Radcliffe, or Cal Tech. Today, admissions committees at selective colleges look at SAT scores, grades, academic program, and evidence of unusual nonacademic talents before they look at the high school the student attended. However, if everything else is equal, the parents' belief that the school attended may tilt the balance in favor of the candidate appears to have some basis in fact. The influence of the school attended is minor compared to its influence in the past, but it is still present. For example, in the 1930s, 1940s, and 1950s, between 90 and 100 percent of the Exeter students who applied to Harvard were admitted. In the 1970s, only 40 to 50 percent of the Exeter applicants were accepted by Harvard. Obviously, although the balance has changed, the odds on being accepted by Harvard are greater in a school like Exeter than an average high school.

Even more impressive are the *overall* records of the elite schools in placing their graduates in selective and very selective colleges. For example, a recent report about the colleges attended by graduates of Andover in the 1970s showed that approximately 40 percent were placed in one of the Ivy League colleges; 20 percent were placed in smaller, but excellent liberal arts colleges such as Amherst, Dartmouth, Swarthmore, and Wesleyan; 5 percent were placed in first class engineering schools, such as Cal Tech, MIT, and RPI; and 10 percent were placed in prestigious universities, such as Berkeley, Duke, Johns Hopkins, and Northwestern. The remaining 25 percent were enrolled in a variety of institutions including private colleges such as Union College, Hobart, and Bard College; private universities such as Boston University, Syracuse, and the University of Southern California; and public colleges such as the University of Georgia, the University of Maine, and Washington State University.

The placement of students in "good" to "highly selective" colleges is very important to the schools because their placement performance impresses parents who are considering the schools. Of course, the placement of students is important to current students and their parents who have paid a lot of money for their children's education. The eyes of students, parents, and prospective students and their parents are all on the schools' successes in placing their students; they all expect the schools to do well. Of course, we have no idea how many of these students would have gone to selective colleges if they had not attended elite schools. The students were bright, ambitious, and academically oriented, so most of them would have gone to college in any case. However, this "what if . . ." possibility seldom occurs to the people in the schools or parents.

Needless to add, the schools take the job of college admissions very seriously. In most of the elite schools, one or two full-time people and one to several part-time people work at college admissions. Although it starts informally much earlier, this work usually formally begins in the junior year, when students are reminded that they should take the SAT examinations in the spring. The schools also encourage parents to take their children to the college campuses they are considering at that time. During the junior and senior year students talk to recruiting representatives from a wide variety of colleges. The schools help their students make realistic choices of colleges, by giving them informed feedback about their academic performance and their chances for admission to the colleges they are considering. Students are encouraged to apply to several institutions they would prefer to enter, with one or two or more "backup" institutions they would be willing to attend if their first choices fall through. Parents usually accept the schools' evaluations and recommendations, but occasionally parents are upset by the schools' estimates (or subsequent rejections by colleges). Some of these parents feel that they paid the schools to get their son or daughter into Yale or Princeton, and they want to see results.

In the students' senior year, most schools check on their progress to make sure that the students have taken care of all the formal application technicalities. In addition, many schools prepare confidential reports, based on teacher, counselor, and housemaster ratings which may help the student get into the college of his or her choice.

Obviously the schools work hard to get each student into the best possible school for him or her. What may be lost in this description is the extent of individual effort for each student. The admissions counselors do not merely give the students the right papers and forms. They seek to find the most *appropriate* college for each student. They talk to students, work with them, and counsel them, so that the students will choose colleges which best fit their own talents and interests. Teachers, housemasters, coaches, and administrators also go to considerable lengths to help students choose the best college. Their efforts range from informal conversations through writing letters of recommendation, to intense personal counseling. In short, the independent schools try to help their students attend good colleges not only because a good placement record is important in attracting new students, but because most teachers, counselors, and administrators sincerely believe in the importance of choosing an appropriate college, and, most important, they are concerned with the educational progress of each of their students.

Students' Self-Portraits and Their Reasons for Coming

The general picture of elite school students is of academically-oriented and resourceful adolescents. This is supported by the results of a question which asked them to rate themselves on a variety of traits. The majority of entering students rated themselves as above average on five traits: common sense, general imagination, ability to make friends, self-discipline, and academic ability. They also rated themselves low on three traits: dramatic ability, artistic ability, and musical ability. In brief, students entered independent schools with a fairly high opinion of themselves, particularly in traits that might be described as general soundness. Before these self-descriptions are dismissed as egotistical errors, it is well to remember that just these kinds of self-ratings have been shown to be highly valid as assessments and predictors (e.g., Baird, 1969b).

Students with such evaluations of themselves might be expected to be quite satisfied with themselves. And indeed they are, as shown in the results of another question.[b] The majority of students were satisfied with themselves in fourteen of the fifteen areas we asked them about (the exception was that "only" 44 percent were satisfied with their religious development; 20 percent were dissatisfied and the rest were undecided). Over 70 percent of the students were satisfied with themselves in four areas: "ability to get along with friends of

[b]The comparative results for this question when asked of older students will be described in Chapter 7.

my own sex," "ability to tell right from wrong," "ability to get along with parents," and "ability to get along with teachers." Once again students seem to be describing themselves as the basically sound and reasonable individuals they most likely are.

The picture of students in the elite schools presented in these and earlier figures is that of bright, balanced, highly motivated students from well-to-do and well-educated families. The implication of this picture is that the elite schools start with everything going for them. If they can merely keep the students in the same condition as when they arrived at the schools their graduates should be successes. It also means that the schools may have difficulty demonstrating that they are successful with their students. It is much easier to show changes in students when you begin with mediocre ones than when you begin with exceptional ones.

Why did these students, who probably would be successful in any school, choose to go to the demanding independent schools? One survey question asked new students their reasons for choosing the school they were attending. Their reasons are important, not only in their own right, but also because they will affect the students' expectations of the school and their experiences there. Earlier research has shown that these reasons are related to students' backgrounds as well as their plans, and achievements in school (Richards and Holland, 1965). The reasons students emphasize may later influence what they will feel about the schools. For example, students who choose schools for their assumed practical benefits may tend to be interested only in the training aspects of school and expect to be provided with practical instruction. They may expect detailed answers and feel that courses in English and the humanities are irrelevant to their needs. Other students choosing schools for other kinds of reasons will show different patterns. Our main concern was whether the reasons students choose independent schools are realistically related to the schools' educational goals. The most important question for the schools is whether their classes, social activities, extracurricular activities, and student groups will form school environments consistent with the reasons students choose the schools.

Do students and their families choose the elite schools for reasons which are consistent with the strengths and emphases of the schools? To answer this question, we asked students who were entering the elite schools about their reasons for coming, their hopes and fears concerning the schools, and the experiences they expected to have in their school. The results revealed that the most important reasons (described as important or very important by 40 percent or more of the sample) for choosing independent schools were predominantly academic: "I thought this school would best prepare me for college" (59 percent), "I think this school will help me grow intellectually" (52 percent), "This school will help me get into college" (48 percent), "I think this school offers a wide variety of interesting courses and activities" (46 percent), and "My parents wanted me to go here" (40 percent). Of course, the last reason is probably largely due to academic factors, too.

A number of reasons were considered quite unimportant (rated important or very important by less than one in ten students): "I didn't get into the school I liked best," "I could not get into the school I preferred with my test scores," "My parents could not afford a more expensive school," "I think I can get good grades without working too hard," "I wanted to be in the city," "I wanted to go to a large school," "I wanted to live with my family," "I wanted to be in the country," "My friends are going here," "A teacher advised me to go here," "I will be able to follow my religious beliefs here," and "This school has fewer rules than others."

The results for several other reasons, which were not rejected so strongly, are also interesting because they go against some of the folklore about independent schools. The first two form an interesting pair, since both are believed to be important by different people: "It is close to home," chosen by 17 percent of the students and "I wanted to live away from home," chosen by 18 percent. Apparently most students neither wish to escape from home by going to independent boarding schools as one theory would have it, nor are they so wedded to their families that they are afraid to "really" leave the nest, as another theory would have it.

Another pair of reasons casts doubt on the idea that the schools are designed to educate an aristocratic elite who will form a coalition later. "One of my parents or relatives went here," was chosen as a reason by only 12 percent of the students. Kraushaar's results show that very few students attend the same independent school their parents did. In fact, nearly 80 percent of independent school parents attended *public* schools. The reason, "I think I will meet people here that will help me in later life," was chosen by 23 percent of the students. Twenty-three percent is not negligible, but compared to academic reasons for attending independent schools, and compared to the results the folklore would suggest, it is a fairly minor reason.

Another story in the folklore is that independent schools catch the students fleeing from poor public schools rife with dissention, drugs, and dumb teachers. In fact, only 22 percent of the new students say they came to independent schools because they thought the schools where they lived were poor. It seems much more plausible, then, that students and their parents are attracted to independent schools largely for academic reasons and are seldom driven into them by fear of the public schools. Kraushaar also found that most parents he asked had chosen to send their children to independent schools for such academically important reasons as the smaller classes, better teachers, and better training in study habits they believe an independent school education provides. Relatively few parents chose independent schools for an "atmosphere free from problems of drugs, delinquency, or turmoil."

The pattern of reasons for students' decisions to attend independent schools suggests that students and their parents are primarily attracted to the schools for the quality of their educational preparation for college. The elite schools still seem to project an image of academic quality. (The schools try to promote this image, not only by listing the colleges attended by their graduates, but by listing the college from which their *faculty* obtained *their* degrees.) The general public seems to believe that private schools provide a better education, according to a recent Gallup poll. The students and parents who come to the schools seem to place a high value on educational excellence and are attracted by the schools' academic strengths.

Student and Parental Hopes

Students and their parents hope to gain many things from their schools, ranging from improvement of their earning potential to the development of their aesthetic appreciation. Of course their hopes are tied to their reasons for choosing the school and their expectations of it. Their hopes may also have strong effects on their educational careers and on their schools.

One question in our survey was directly concerned with what students hoped they would gain from independent school. The items were designed to provide a profile of students' expectations for educational and personal growth and of the things they feel would result in a satisfying educational career. (The specific items parallel those in a similar question described in Chapter 7 and are based on the same conception of developmental tasks.) Some of the results students hope for are chiefly personal, such as improving self-confidence and learning to accept responsibility, and may be difficult for the school to affect in a direct way. Others, such as knowing about national or international politics and improving one's ability to think, may be indirectly amenable to the efforts of the school. Finally, a number of hopes—for example, acquiring knowledge and skill in English and learning how to be creative in the performing or fine arts—have direct relations with the schools' characteristics, particularly the curriculum.

When students were asked what they hoped to get from their independent school education by the time they finished, three things stood out: "To be prepared for college" (chosen by 72 percent), "To improve my ability to think" (61 percent), and "To learn to accept responsibility" (52 percent). Each of these results was "strongly" hoped for by over half the students. Thus, the students hope to gain just those things on which these schools pride themselves.

In contrast, four goals were not particularly important to 40 percent or more of the students: "To learn more about my religion" (54 percent said "Don't care"), "To get ready for marriage and family life" (46 percent don't care), "To learn how to be creative in the performing or fine arts" (42 percent don't care), and "To be able to appreciate art such as music, painting, and other work" (41 percent don't care). Thus, religion, art, and preparation for marriage are not the primary focus of the hopes of the students; rather, traditional academic goals seem to predominate their thinking. In Chapter 7, we will examine twelfth graders' judgments about their progress toward the same goals.

Parents' Hopes

Much has been written about parental pressures on students, whether in the form of direct coercion or psychological influence. The traditional family has been criticized as the primary source of neurosis, guilt, and deviancy. The same charges have been leveled at the "new" family which, supposedly following the invidious advice of Dr. Spock, has been accused of leading children to become haughty, spoiled, neurotic protestors. Both of these views seem to be cartoon exaggerations of trends that are part of a changing society, and neither seem to accurately reflect the diversity, resiliency, and adaptability of the American family.

This book is not a study of the family, but everyone must recognize the critical importance of parental pressures and hopes for students' educational careers. The families of the students who enter the elite schools are committed to educational excellence as evidenced by the fact that they seek out the schools and are willing to pay high tuitions in order to obtain the best education for their children. As we pointed out earlier, Kraushaar's results also show that the parents of independent school students choose independent schools predominantly for academic reasons.

We have already seen that the families of the elite school students have unusually high social and educational status and seem to have strong personal commitments to academic excellence. They also seem to make their desires apparent to their children, as seen in the results for a survey question which deals with parental hopes for their children's behavior. Parental expectations and values have a strong influence on the values and behavior of secondary school students. The survey question was designed to provide information about the kinds of behavior parents expect their children to exhibit. Moreover, it provides information about what parents expect from the schools. If students do not meet their parents' hopes, they may be disappointed and begin pressuring them. They may also question the efforts of the school and try to bring pressure to bear on it. By providing indirect information about the values of parents, the answers to this question may also suggest whether parents would support the schools' efforts in certain areas.

The question asked new students to indicate how strongly they thought their parents felt about their behavior in thirteen areas. The results showed that, as reported by the students, parental hopes seem to mirror those of their children. According to 90 percent or more of the students, their parents want them to stay in school, learn to think for themselves, and go on to college well prepared for the academic demands they will face there. Three-fourths of the students think their parents do not care if they win a prize in art or music, or act in a school play. (The results for another question showed that most entering students have no personal interest in art clubs or musical activities.) Thus, both students and their parents seem to be more interested in the academic benefits of the schools than in their preparation for adult roles or their emphasis on such expressive activities as art and music.

Worries and Expectations

Students and their parents have many hopes for the schools, but this is just part of the story. Students entering the elite schools also have concerns and worries about their schools. The age at which most students enter the elite schools is an age of uncertainty and anxiety. In addition, the boarding school experience adds such problems as living away from home or adjusting to school rules. However, it turned out that entering students were not concerned about these possible problems.

The results for one question reflect the academic concerns shown in the results for other questions. It was not surprising to find that the majority of students expected to "need to improve my study habits" (68 percent), and to "feel a lot of pressure to get good grades" (56 percent). The things the majority of students felt would *not* be true were more instructive: They felt they would not be bothered by "having to take part in the physical education or athletic program," by the "lack of privacy," "the isolation of the school," the "religious requirements of the school," and thought they would not "have trouble finding friends." They also did not expect to be troubled by "school rules," or "living away from home," and did not feel they would "need help in choosing courses." Students generally did not have negative expectations.

It is striking that the new students did not anticipate the complaints of older students about the lack of privacy, isolation of the schools, and the narrowness of rules, which will be described in later chapters.

What do new students expect their independent school experience to be like? Students' expectations of the school environment are, of course, related to their hopes for the school and their reasons for choosing it, but are also related to their adjustment to it. Their expectations are a gauge of how well they really know the school and understand it. Some research has shown that when entering students have erroneous views of what a school is like, they tend to be less satisfied, have more adjustment problems, and may be more likely to drop out.

We asked students for their perception of aspects of the schools that have been found to be important for distinguishing among institutions. Most of the items reflect perceptions of the climate or atmosphere of the school and consequently show how students feel about the schools they are entering. These feelings may reveal deeper, more subtle expectations. We felt that the results of this question could be useful in understanding the image the schools are projecting and the kind of schools the students expect to find. The results showed that the students had a very *positive* image of the schools. Seventy percent or more of the students expected the students and teachers to be friendly, the teaching to be good, the athletic and extracurricular programs to be good, and that the school would stimulate students to think. Further, the majority clearly did *not* think students are treated like numbers.

Students' views were less clear about whether there is an active social life, whether the school emphasized religion, whether rules are strictly enforced, and whether there is a lot of competition for grades. It is odd that students thought they would feel a lot of pressure to get good grades, but were less certain about the level of competition. They were also sure that the school would be friendly, but were uncertain about the social life. In spite of these contradictions students generally foresaw few problems. They expected a warm and stimulating school environment.

One factor that complicates the results is that many students, no matter what the school is really like, tend to have an ideal image of all high schools: friendly, stimulating, sociable, and filled with interesting things to do. The results should thus be interpreted with caution, since students may be describing the ideal rather than the actual schools they are entering.

Summary

The picture of the new students presented by these results is one of bright, balanced and alert students from good homes. They are academically oriented, but are not too concerned about opportunities for developing or expressing their creativity. They expect their new schools to stimulate them and foster the growth of their abilities. Perhaps the greatest challenge to the schools is to live up to these expectations. When we compare the bright-eyed, eager entering students with many of their disillusioned, cynical or hostile senior peers, one must ask whether this transition is due to the students, to society, or whether it is due to the inability or unwillingness of the schools to meet the great expectations of the students. We will return to this topic in later chapters.

3

The Life of the Students in the Schools

Is there anything unusual about the life of the students in the elite schools of the 1970s? There are many answers to this question, some found in history, some in the backgrounds of the students, and some in the nature of the schools. The first answer lies in the changing concept of "youth." It is surprising that the very idea of childhood and adolescence is historically relatively recent. Throughout most of man's history children were simply considered to be small adults (Aries, 1962). In particular, only in the nineteenth century did people begin to believe that there was a special period of adolescence that required special provisions. The role of the school has changed in correspondence with these changing conceptions of youth. Originally the schools were primarily concerned with providing students with basic reading, writing, and arithmetical skills and other pieces of knowledge that were regarded as useful for particular social roles. As the requirements of these same roles came to demand further education, the elite schools changed from the preparation of students for social roles, to the preparation of students for more preparation (see McLachlan, 1970 for an historical account of the changing nature of the schools).

In the contemporary world, the elite schools find their role of helping students to mature a difficult one because of the difficulties of today's adolescents. However, it is easy to exaggerate the problems of growing up in our society. The stress, turmoil, and unhappiness that so many writers have emphasized is much less common than they would lead us to believe. Studies indicate that most youth go through adolescence without major trauma. Still, there are many difficulties in youth that are part of almost every student's life. First, of course, youth are basically dependent on their parents and the social system. This dependence has been lessened through changing childrearing patterns, particularly among upper and upper middle class families, which, as we have seen are the most likely to send their children to the elite schools (Bronfenbrenner, 1970). Childrearing patterns have changed from the use of coercion to the use of persuasion and manipulation. There is much greater tolerance of the child's impulses and wishes and freer expression of affection and anger. Discipline is more "psychological," depending on reasoning and appeals to the child's conscience. At the same time youth have been given much more freedom of choice and wider latitude in their activities. These trends seem to hold most strongly among upper middle class families which leads to the second answer to the question at the beginning of this chapter.

Even with the freedom and indulgence allowed by their families, youth are

21

treated like a minority, as Matza (1964) has pointed out. When the condition of minorities improves, but when they also are still basically treated as second-class citizens, the result is a rising expectation for more freedom, and a lowered sense of personal position. This pattern also seems to hold for youth. The adolescents who have gained greater freedom of action and expression often wish for even more. They are also unsure of the limits of their social position, unsure whether they are independent adults or children to be controlled. One of the consequences of this ambiguity is that both youth and adults are uncertain about what constitutes proper behavior among youth. Because the adults are unsure of the behaviors they can demand of youth and because they suspect that youth are not quite mature, they are sometimes touchy in dealing with them. The adolescent often counters this with a show of youthful defiance, partly due to the youth's resentment of being reminded that many of the rights he assumes are really indulgences. The strains and tensions of many interactions between the youth and adults are the result. All of these tendencies are exacerbated when final "adult" status can only be gained by achievement, performance, and proper conduct, rather than by simply growing older. For example, consider the pressures on those students who are told they must get good grades so they may get into a good college so they may get into a good graduate or professional school so they may get into a good career so they may finally be considered adequate adults. It is not surprising that some students would rebel against such definitions of their lives and engage in deviant or delinquent behavior. Another reaction is for students to turn to other students in the same position for mutual help and sympathy. These historical and social trends, then, are one source of the nature of student life in the elite schools.

A third influence on student friendships and groupings lies in the nature of the schools themselves. All schools have assumed more and more of the responsibilities once held by parents by their programs of extracurricular activities, social events, counseling and health facilities, guidance for college and careers, and more. The elite schools add physical isolation and, in most cases, bread and board. In essence, the schools separate students from the rest of adult society. The result is that students turn inward to the school and their peers. But the adult world has organized the schools, and the schools reflect its values. The scholastic system, in particular, stems directly from the adult society. The pressures of the academic system lead students to look to each other and thus to the formation of student subgroups.

Let us now draw all these ideas together and apply them to bright, privileged, and relatively autonomous students from homes which allowed them considerable latitude in action and expression, who then enter a social system (the school) that is largely isolated from society, which has many demands and traditions of its own, along with many other students quite similar to themselves in background and outlook. The formation of active subgroups based on a "student culture" would seem almost inevitable.

Some Evidence of the Importance of Student Life

One may concede all the points in the last section yet still doubt the importance of students to one another in the school. After all, one might ask, doesn't the school itself play a preeminent role in the growth of students, and haven't you emphasized the total immersion of the student in the life of the school? It would seem, then, that the various agencies of the school would have as much to do with a student's life as other students.

The evidence we have seems to run counter to this argument; in most areas students do seem to look to one another before they look to adults. For example, when we asked students to tell us who or what were the most important sources of their ethical or spiritual values, they most often (60 percent) said "student friends." Parents, with 55 percent, and reading, with 45 percent, were the only other sources frequently mentioned. Teachers were considered a source of values only by 21 percent; the other potential sources in the school such as the clergy or counselors fared even more poorly. It is striking that teachers and administrators also thought student friends were the most important sources of values for most students, but assigned much more importance to their own efforts than did the students.

A second piece of evidence for the importance of student society may seem a little further afield. We asked students to rate the importance of various influences on their standards of sexual behavior. Only two influences were described as important or very important by a majority: "friends my own age" by 60 percent, and "parents" by 52 percent. Such school related influences as teachers, school counselors, and ministers, rabbis or clergymen were rated as unimportant or very unimportant by over two-thirds of the students.

The final piece of evidence comes from a question designed to assess the counseling facilities in the schools, which will be discussed in Chapter 4. Students were asked to whom they would first turn if they felt they needed help in certain areas. Students indicated they would most likely turn to another student in four of the most critical areas: trouble in adjusting to the school, personal problems, drugs, and relations with the opposite sex. They would most often turn to their parents when choosing occupations, finding jobs, and solving financial problems. They said they would turn to teachers if they had problems with classwork or reading or study skills, and they would turn to counselors for advice about college admission. Otherwise students said they would seldom turn to teachers, school counselors, house or dormitory masters, doctors, clergymen or any other adult. The point is that, except for strictly academic advice, few students would turn to adults in the school. For their most intimate problems, they would turn to other students.

When students do turn to one another, what do they find; what is the nature of these student relationships? Much has been written about the "adolescent society" that extends across the nation and helps form the student subculture in our secondary schools (Clark, 1962). In the 50s the ingredients of the adolescent society were supposed to consist of rock n' roll, dating, cars, clothes, and athletics. In the 70s it is supposed to consist of just plain rock, long hair, blue jeans, marijuana and an antimaterialistic view of life that has been called a new level of consciousness (Reich, 1971). The only things that have stayed the same in these pictures are the influence of the mass media, rock music, conformity to peer expectations, and a kind of anti-intellectualism. These descriptions have become cliches and one may wonder whether the cliches are true. A number of researchers (Elkin and Westley, 1955; Remmers and Radler, 1957; Turner, 1964) have found little support for the descriptions. In fact, Turner has wondered to what extent that which passes as youth culture is the "line" used by mass media hucksters to address youthful audiences rather than the spontaneous behavior of youth itself. In particular, one may wonder how this characterization applies to independent schools, since the students are generally academically oriented, make independent judgments, and come from high status homes.

Some observers have suggested that there is not one, but several types of student subculture. Clark (1962), for example, contends that there are four subcultures: (1) the fun subculture, with an emphasis on pleasure and social success, (2) the academic subculture, with an emphasis on achievement, (3) the delinquent subculture, with an emphasis on rejection of adult demands and (4) rebellious intellectuals with an emphasis on independence and ideas. Clark believes that only the first three are found in most schools, and that the academic subculture is usually weak, if not absent. In the independent schools one would expect more students in academic and rebellious intellectual subgroups because of the nature of the schoools and the background of the students.

We attempted to assess the character of student life in independent schools and to assess the validity of the various ideas about student subgroups as they apply to independent school students in two ways. In the first, we asked the people in the schools about the sources of status among students, and in the second we asked them to identify the student leaders in the schools. The sources of status among students are important for several reasons. They reflect the basis of social attraction and influence among students. They indicate the characteristics that students value, and they suggest the kinds of persons who may become leaders. In this study we tried to assess the sources of status among independent school students by asking them (and teachers and administrators) to indicate the importance of various characteristics in order for a student to "be looked up to" by other students at their schools. The results in Table 3-1 show that a majority of students described four characteristics as clearly unimportant: "have plenty of money," "come from a good family," "break rules," and "know a lot about movies, TV, and popular music." "Be a rebel," "be a student activist," "know a lot about literature and the arts," and "make high grades" also received rather

Table 3-1
Sources of Status Among Students
(in percentages)

| | Group | | | | | | | | |
| | Students | | | Teachers | | | Administrators | | |
Source	U*	S	V	U	S	V	U	S	V
Come from a good family	64	24	6	50	36	5	63	27	1
Be a leader in extracurricular activities	18	51	26	6	54	34	5	52	36
Have plenty of money	67	21	7	52	33	5	62	27	1
Make high grades	37	48	12	22	58	14	12	65	14
Be an athlete or cheerleader	32	43	20	20	54	17	18	57	18
Know a lot about literature and arts	48	41	6	40	44	6	31	54	4
Know what's going on in national and international politics	30	49	16	23	53	13	25	52	15
Know a lot about movies, TV, and popular music	50	37	8	31	46	10	39	41	8
Be a rebel	46	36	10	37	40	8	43	38	8
Have a good personality	3	20	73	3	23	68	1	27	64
Have a good moral character	26	38	30	15	49	26	10	45	39
Be popular with the opposite sex	30	41	22	27	44	9	25	49	11
Be an open, friendly person	6	24	67	2	31	62	2	28	63
Be a student activist	36	37	19	38	41	6	43	37	8
Break rules	61	23	9	56	23	3	59	20	1

Source: *Questionnaire for Students, Teachers and Administrators* and *Questionnaire for New Students*, Educational Testing Service and the Secondary School Research Program, © 1971, 1972, Educational Testing Service.
*U = Unimportant; S = Somewhat important; V = Very important; Not shown = Can't say and no response
The item read as follows: (to be answered by everyone) In order to be looked up to by other students at your school, how important is it for a student to do or be each of the following?

low ratings. Only two characteristics were described as very important by a majority of students: "be an open, friendly person," and "have a good personality." No other characteristic of the fifteen was considered nearly as important. (The views of teachers and administrators were generally about the same, although there were slight differences on some items.) It is noteworthy that the same two characteristics were the only ones described by a majority of students as important on another question about being popular with the opposite sex; furthermore, about the same characteristics which were *unimportant* in being looked up to were unimportant in being popular with the opposite sex. It is striking that no intellectual or academic characteristics were seen as highly important. It is also striking that athletes and cheerleaders were not guaranteed status. The sources of status among students, then, seem to center about a general trait of sociability. One student expressed this, while denying the premise of the question. "I don't think it is at all important to be looked up to!! I think it is important to be friendly, and have a good personality, to get along with people." Other students pointed out that "students are so varied that they admire other students for different things and in different degrees" and that "there are different kinds of 'in' crowds where values and attitudes are in opposing directions." Other students rejected some of the possible items: "Personally, I don't look up to any other student because he has good grades or a smart mouth . . . this isn't 1955 in the college dorm." Other students suggested other sources of status; for example, "students seem to me to admire students who are strongly interested in and good at *something*—but not necessarily any of the things mentioned." And finally, a student pointed out the need for questions about the sources of status "you would like to see changed."

No matter what the sources of status among elite school students, they seem to be fairly unconcerned about status generally. In another question "being in or out with certain groups of students" bothered fewer students than almost any other potential source of stress. Teachers and administrators were much more likely to think students were bothered by being "in or out."

We also tried to obtain information about a related area, student leadership. The choice of leaders may reflect the values of individual students, the things the school rewards, and the power relations in a school. We therefore asked students, teachers, and administrators to indicate "which kinds of students actually exercise leadership" at their school. Respondents marked two groups from a list of ten. They could also indicate that there were no real student leaders. Some 17 percent of students, 7 percent of teachers, and 5 percent of the administrators did indicate there were no real student leaders. Among the other choices, only three were chosen by as many as 20 percent of the persons in the study: first, "elected or appointed class officers or student body officers," second, "leaders of student activities," and third, "the all-around students." Overall, high grade-getters, political activists, rebels, creative students, and students successful in out of school activities were less frequently indicated as leaders.

A number of students commented on this question and pointed out that there are many kinds of leaders for many kinds of groups: "The school leaders are a variety of people, ranging from the town meeting (student gov't) to the head of the religious association to the team leaders." Comment about the character of leaders ranged from "there is very little effective student leadership at all" and "the only people who exercise leadership are the administration flunkies," to "anyone who really desires to can exercise some force of leadership" and "almost everyone is a leader in some way at our school." Some students felt the need to explain the situation at their school at length. For example:

The term "leader" can be interpreted in many and different ways. I answered the question not to my definition of a "leader," but as the school would define a "leader." This would mainly refer to the cliques such as Student Council, cheerleaders, etc. The problem is that the students who are on Student Council are all of a certain type and most of them really aren't that interested in the world as a whole. A so-called "hippie" would *never* have a chance at this school to be on Student Council etc., although he does have the opportunity to run. This school (as students go) is far too conservative and does not really get involved in affairs such as pollution etc.

The responses to the questions on status and leadership suggest that the student culture in independent schools is more complex than any of the ideas outlined at the beginning of this chapter would suggest. A walk on any campus provides convincing evidence for the influence of a national youth style, if not a "culture." The music, clothing, grooming, posters, and topics of conversation are much the same almost everywhere. (The exceptions, of course, are the handful of schools which retain conservative dress and grooming rules.) But it is difficult to demonstrate that this constitutes a "culture." There is still a great deal of diversity among students, almost as much as in the adult world. One may also wonder if the ubiquitous music and dress is a true outgrowth of a youth culture or if it primarily is a symbolic basis for students' attraction to one another and for their relations with adults. The presence of shared tastes, particularly if they are immediately visible, makes friendships much easier to form (Newcomb, 1961). Shared interests and tastes then tend to cement the friendships and groups that are formed. Thus, the national youth style influences students indirectly, by helping students relate to each other. The influence may be quite shallow in many areas, however. Student attitudes and general outlooks on life are probably much less influenced by the national style than one would expect. It may at first seem incongruous to hear a long-haired and mustachioed student in blue jeans say that we should have A-bombed North Vietnam back to the Stone Age, but it really shouldn't be too surprising. Most students' ideas are still largely formed by their backgrounds, whatever the patina they get from the national culture.

Our results also do not support the other ideas of the importance of athletics, money, cars, or clothes. The earlier studies, which found that these things were important among students, used public school samples, and were conducted in the 1950s. Values have changed since the 50s, and independent schools have always differed from others.

None of Clark's four types of subcultures described at the beginning of this chapter—the fun, academic, delinquent, and rebellious intellectual subcultures—appear in the forms Clark described in the elite schools. Of course, the schools themselves are so heavily committed—one might even say lopsided in their devotion—to academic achievement that it would almost be redundant for students to relate to one another in that way. In most of the elite schools most of the students are oriented toward academic achievement. Thus, any subgroups that form in the elite schools are sub-subgroups within an academic subculture. The divisions and groupings among students going to college and students going to work are not part of the elite schools—virtually all plan to go to college and all are academic. For the same reason there is virtually no delinquent subgroup. The friendliness that seems the key to elite school student relationships also does not seem to be really akin to a "fun" subculture. Perhaps most surprising is the relative lack of rebellious intellectual subgroups, although the students' values, as we shall see in Chapter 6, are concerned with being independent and original and with standing up for their own rights. Apparently students' *individual* values do not form a basis for group values. To put this point a little differently, students very probably seek different things from other students than confirmation of their own values. In any case, it seems that none of the approaches to student groups that were outlined at the beginning of the chapter apply very well to the elite school students.

Attraction Between the Sexes

The elite schools seem to simultaneously exhibit a denial of sex and an obsession with sex. The single sex schools, by their very essence, represent an attempt to segregate sex out of student experience. The coeducational boarding schools demonstrate their concern for sex by their thickets of rules and restrictions. Part of this concern is no doubt because the schools must serve *in loco parentis*, and would be considered morally, if not legally, liable if a student got into sexual difficulty. But there is a much more fundamental reason for the schools' concern with sex: the students who come to the schools are entering the stage of life when they must come to terms with their own growing sexuality and with their ability to deal with sexual feelings and relations. Consider the physiological changes that a twelve or thirteen year old will go through before the end of his or her senior year. First the girls. There is a spurt in height and weight; breasts begin to develop and enlarge; pubic hair appears; the body chemistry changes; the body, and the girl's conception of her body, change; and menstruation begins. Boys, too, face a spurt in height and weight; facial and pubic hair appear; hormones change, the penis and testes increase in size; and the capacity for sexual functioning is established. As the students go through these physiological changes they try to deal with them psychologically, and as students change within the schools, the schools must deal with the changes, at least informally. Some schools try hard to help students cope with new feelings and ideas, some have counseling programs, and some hope that the housemasters or housemistresses will be able to cope with students' sexuality, but none can deny the seriousness of the task, whether they care to tackle it or not.

The psychological concerns that students face in sex have always been great, but are perhaps even greater today. The worries about masturbation, fears of homosexuality, moral agonies about premarital intercourse, and fears of pregnancy are all tied to the adolescents' growing sense of themselves and their emotions. Journalistic accounts make it appear that the "sexual revolution" results in easy, relaxed, sincere sexual experiences. But, as teachers and counselors who work closely with students know, students are still worried and anxious about sex, perhaps more so because of the talk of permissiveness. Many adolescents may not be psychologically or socially ready for sexual experiences, but may feel pressure to proceed. In an odd way permissiveness may turn out to be the opposite for young people who would prefer to proceed in their relations to each other at their own rate and in their own way. The images of a permissive and promiscuous youth may pressure the student who is not ready for such behavior to engage in it. Of course, many, if not most, students grow up in homes that fostered the traditional beliefs about sex and marriage, and are consequently torn between traditional and permissive ideas. Adolescents have the difficult task of charting their own course between these poles, working out their own way without simply obeying outworn conventions or following the newer conventions of a swinging society.

The schools, in their role as surrogate parents, face a task nearly as difficult as that of the students when they try to help students find their own way. Beyond the difficulties of helping students themselves, the schools have other problems. Parents may expect the schools to preach the traditional approaches to sex. Some parents may think the school should do nothing. The administrators and teachers may be divided in their own views about how to help students come to terms with sexuality, some being quite conservative, some being liberal. All of these pressures and divisions make it harder for schools to effectively help students reach a realistic and responsible maturity. Rather than giving either easy "thou shalt not" or "anything goes" advice, the schools seeking an adult approach to sex need to help their students repeatedly ask themselves "Am I being honest with myself? Will this behavior harm me or those I love? Will it be good for me? and Is this really what I want?"

Even when they are not having to deal with such weighty questions girls and boys have to deal with each other. They are learning to enjoy each others' companionship, exploring the diversity among the members of the opposite sex, and trying to find ways to reach a feeling of intimacy and care for each other. Because of the limitations of the survey technique, we could not adequately explore students' growing competency in interpersonal relations or their increasing depth and maturity of personality. We could, however, study the areas of student development that the schools could conceivably do something about, or which a student might come to a counselor about. Accordingly we examined the sources of students' sexual values, the sources of attraction between students of the opposite sex, evaluations of the opportunities to meet the opposite sex, and students' wishes for help in coping with relations between the sexes.

Students' Standards of Sexual Behavior

According to various popular explanations, students' (presumably poor) standards of sexual behavior are strongly influenced by television, sexy movies, and *Playboy* magazine. However, as shown in Table 3-2, when the students in this study were asked to describe the importance of various people and media as sources of their personal standards concerning sexual behavior, only two very traditional ones were described as important by a majority: their parents and friends of their own age. *Every* other source but one in the list of eleven was described as unimportant or very unimportant by a majority of students. (The one exception was brothers or sisters described as unimportant by 44 percent.) Four sources were described as unimportant by two-thirds or more of the students: school counselors, television, teachers, and ministers, rabbis, and clergymen. Four other sources were also described as unimportant: books, movies and plays, other adults, and magazines or newspapers. It appears that students generally report the same sources of sexual standards that people always have: parents and peers. The school seems to play a very small role in the development of these standards.

Table 3-2
Sources of Students' Standards of Sexual Behavior
(in percentages)

	Response		
Source	*U**	*I*	*V*
Friends of my own age	29	41	19
Brothers or sisters	44	25	10
Books	56	23	5
Movies and plays	64	18	3
Parents	36	34	18
Teachers	71	11	3
School counselors	73	6	2
Minister, rabbi, clergyman	68	9	3
Other adults	57	22	4
Television	73	10	1
Magazines, newspapers	64	18	3

Source: *Questionnaire for Students, Teachers, and Administrators* and *Questionnaire for New Students*, Educational Testing Service and the Secondary School Research Program, © 1971, 1972, Educational Testing Service.

*U = Very unimportant or Unimportant; I = Important; V = Very important; Not shown = Can't say, Doesn't apply, No response

The item read as follows: (students only) How important are each of the following sources of your own personal standards concerning sexual behavior?

Students' comments were very much in line with the picture presented by the responses to the questions. One student asked: "What relation can newspapers, or plays have on my sexual behavior?" and another asked "What do you mean books, TV, newspapers? Articles on what happens, etc., can help; dirty books, etc., don't even influence my desire." Another student explained what "friends of my own age" means:

I feel the need to clarify my answer of friends of my age being important. Important open discussion of sexual behavior, premarital sex, and other somewhat "liberal" views of sex which I could not discuss point blank with my parents. I do not feel "peer pressure" as far as having or not having sexual relationships.

The sources of attraction between students of opposite sex are many and vary with each individual and with each relationship. But the bases for attraction are a great concern for many adolescents, and often a source of worry to parents and teachers. These bases often form the background for interpersonal experiences that have a bearing on later choices culminating in the choice of a person to share one's life with. The sources of attraction between the sexes, then, are psychologically and socially important, and were assessed in this study by asking students to rate the importance of sixteen characteristics for a student to be popular with the opposite sex. Teachers and administrators were also asked their opinions about the importance of the characteristics.

As shown in Table 3-3, only two characteristics were described as very important by the majority of students (or adults): "have a good personality" and "be an open, friendly person." Only two other characteristics were described as very important by as many as 12 percent of the students: "have a good moral character" with 35 percent and "be physically attractive" with 31 percent. In contrast, eight characteristics were described as unimportant by a clear majority of students: "come from a good family," "know a lot about books and literature," "have plenty of money," "make high grades," "be a student activist," "be a far-out dresser," "be a rebel," and "break rules." There were differences between the perceptions of male and female students. Somewhat more of the boys thought that "having a lot of money" and "being an athlete or cheerleader" were more important than did girls. Somewhat more of the girls thought that "knowing what's going on in national and international politics" was important than did males. These differences may reflect the somewhat greater self-confidence of adolescent girls compared to adolescent boys reported in many research studies. The less confident boys may tend to exaggerate the importance of external characteristics.

Teachers and administrators generally rated the importance of the characteristics about the same way that students did, except that they thought several characteristics were more important than did students, particularly having plenty of money, being a leader in extracurricular activities, and knowing a lot about movies, TV, and popular music. The difference in perception concerning

Table 3-3

Views of the Factors Involved in Popularity with the Opposite Sex Among Students

(in percentages)

Factor	Group Students U*	S	V	Teachers U	S	V	Administrators U	S	V
Be physically attractive	5	57	31	4	52	36	4	62	28
Make high grades	62	27	2	57	29	1	66	22	1
Have plenty of money	58	26	4	37	41	6	50	36	1
Be an athlete or cheerleader	49	34	9	37	41	8	39	47	3
Come from a good family	51	31	6	40	37	6	50	34	3
Be a leader in extracurricular activities	44	39	6	26	53	6	27	62	6
Know a lot about books and literature	52	34	4	50	34	1	45	40	1
Know what's going on in national and international politics	38	43	10	33	46	7	32	55	5
Know a lot about movies, TV, and popular music	36	46	9	13	57	17	16	58	17
Be a student activist	57	25	5	44	33	3	51	26	3
Break rules	72	13	3	58	18	2	68	19	1
Be a rebel	69	15	4	53	22	2	65	20	1
Have a good personality	2	9	83	1	17	74	0	18	77
Have a good moral character	17	37	35	16	48	18	9	64	17
Be an open, friendly person	3	13	78	1	24	66	1	22	71
Be a far-out dresser	69	16	3	53	23	2	53	25	1

Source: *Questionnaire for Students, Teachers and Administrators* and *Questionnaire for New Students*, Educational Testing Service and the Secondary School Research Program, © 1971, 1972, Educational Testing Service.

*U = Unimportant; S = Of some importance; V = Very important. Percentages for "Can't say" and no response are not shown.

The item read as follows:

Students—In order to be popular with the opposite sex, how important is it for a student to do or be the following?

Teachers and administrators—In order for students to be popular with the opposite sex, how important do you think it is for them to do or be the following?

extracurricular activities is probably due to the adults' belief that the school and its extracurriculum is important to students and their view of students as immature.

The number of comments about these questions suggest the importance and complexity of interpersonal relations between the sexes among students. One theme in the comments was that the answers depend on the persons involved. One student noted "... there are various different groups in the school which have different likes and dislikes." Another student commented: "It depends on who your friends are, the type of person you are and they are." And another: "... the reasons for an individual's response to another vary. In one case, for example, a person's athletic ability might contribute to his popularity, but, in another, his athletic talent may have no bearing on his acceptance." A second theme was that students do not try to package themselves for popularity with the opposite sex: "One is not a student activist, rebel or a good student to attract a person of the opposite sex. Also, one does not change one's personality if one is a strong person. . . . I am what I am because I feel that way and will not change to play silly games of attracting the opposite sex." Commented another student: "Most people don't go around changing their personality to appeal to every different person they are attracted to." A third theme was that the subgroups at most schools allowed any kind of person to be popular with at least *some* students. One girl wrote: "One needs 'something' entirely different to appeal to dumb boys than to smart boys, to athletes than to student activists, to intellectuals than to rich snobs, etc." Another student commented: "... the way-out dresser, the rebel, the activist, the against-the-establishment-types are the ones who lead one large group. The other large segment is led by the typical, clean-cut, clean-living, scholar types. Each type is popular in his own way." And another: "... when you are involved in a school such as I am where there is such a wide variety of types of students such an example as 'be a rebel' or 'have plenty of money' could be answered in both extremities."

The Question of Coeducation

One of the most active controversies in many of the elite schools revolves around the question of whether the single sex schools should become coeducational. The traditions of the single sex schools were based on the idea that students' educational and personal growth would be easier when they were not distracted by daily encounters with the opposite sex. The staffs of the schools also believed they could better deal with the special needs of each sex when the schools formed environments especially designed for boys or for girls. Many people in the single sex schools still believe in the value of their special environments. Other people feel that the single sex arrangement is outmoded, unrealistic, and unnatural. Certainly the single sex feature is a source of a good deal of student unhappiness. There seem to be good reasons on each side of the question of coeducation. Not the least of these are the considerations of the uniqueness of the single sex boarding schools in the American educational landscape. Kraushaar has pointed this out in discussing the controversy about coeducation.

What this implies for the future of single sex schools is not altogether clear. A wholesale shift to coeduction would have the regrettable outcome of increasing by that much more the uniformity and standardization of schools at a time when many deplore the lack of diversity and the steady constriction of choices to fewer and fewer really different options. As it is, single sex schools, many with distinguished records, serve as a counter-cyclical force resisting the rush toward the standardization of education in this respect. For many such schools, however, the issue is now or may soon be defined as a struggle for bare survival. Unfortunately, there is no assurance that turning to coeducation is in itself a guarantee of survival. For example, a school for girls that has built a distinguished reputation among its kind could well turn out, in the process of becoming coeducational, to be just another school. But there may be no satisfactory alternative, except perhaps for a small number of prestigious, well-endowed single sex schools that could continue to attract a sufficient number of clients who prefer that kind of an environment or feel they need it. Some students indicated a desire to change from coeducational to single sex schools, and some in single sex schools express satisfaction with their school as it is. But their number is very small. The steady growth of sentiment, over the past century, in favor of coeducational education makes it seem unlikely that the trend will be reversed or arrested in the foreseeable future. Indeed, many traditionally single sex schools of national prominence are now in the process of change to coordinate or coeducation. Yet a number of single sex colleges have let it be known recently that after a careful study of various alternatives they have decided to stand pat in this respect.

When we asked students, teachers, and administrators in the elite schools how satisfied they were with opportunities for students to meet and associate with the opposite sex in various areas, the results, shown in Table 3-4, were clear. The majority of students were dissatisfied with the opportunities in every area. In contrast, teachers and administrators tended to be satisfied with the opportunities. The comments on this question showed that almost all students wanted more opportunities and many in single sex schools wanted their schools to go coed.

A number of other results to be reported more extensively later bear on students' sexual development. For example, students strongly felt their standards of behavior in relations with the opposite sex were well defined, but 65 percent said that they were bothered a little or very much by relations with the opposite sex (males reported they were bothered more often than females). However, only about a third of the students reported that they were dissatisfied with their ability to relate to the opposite sex.

What the Schools Might Do

What do students want from their schools in the area of information or help in sexual relations? Several items reported more fully later bear on this question. First, students were asked if there had been changes in their school recently in

Table 3-4

Satisfaction with Students' Opportunities to Meet the Opposite Sex

(in percentages)

| Opportunities for meeting and associating with the opposite sex in: | Group | | | | | | | | |
| | Students | | | Teachers | | | Administrators | | |
	SD*	D	S	SD	D	S	SD	D	S
Classes	41	14	14	13	20	31	7	22	32
Informal school life	41	21	17	9	26	47	7	30	49
Formal school events	33	22	22	6	18	64	4	20	62
School dances	28	25	28	6	20	62	3	21	65
The local community	35	20	19	10	26	40	6	26	38
Extracurricular activities	35	22	22	7	27	48	7	28	51

Source: *Questionnaire for Students, Teachers and Administrators* and *Questionnaire for New Students*, Educational Testing Service and the Secondary School Research Program, © 1971, 1972, Educational Testing Service.

*SD = Strongly dissatisfied; D = Dissatisfied; S = Satisfied or Strongly satisfied; Not shown = Doesn't apply or no response

The item read as follows: How satisfied are you with the opportunities students have for meeting and associating with members of the opposite sex at your school?

various areas, including sex education. A fairly large percentage (35 percent) of students responded "No, but changes need to be made" in the area of sex education, and 22 percent more responded "Yes, but more change is still needed." Only 11 percent felt the change had been adequate. Another item asked students for their opinions about what their school should provide in the area of relations between the sexes. Some 54 percent said information, 40 percent said counseling, and 40 percent said courses. Only 12 percent said the school should do nothing.

The results reported in this section suggest that the schools have little direct effect on students' growth in sexuality and capacity for intimacy. Students seldom credited any influence on their sexual standards by adults in the school. They seemed to feel that they did not need the advice of adults in the school, and were fairly certain that they had clear standards. However, many felt that their schools should do something to help students relate to each other. Many students also desired more effective sex education programs. The schools seem to need to do much more to help students. In fact, students in single sex schools often feel that their schools are hindering the development of their ability to relate to the opposite sex.

The pressures of the intense environments of the elite schools may influence relations between the sexes in the same way the schools seem to influence student friendships and groups. As suggested earlier, the pressures of the environment may make the need for regard and intimate companionship paramount over other needs. Friendships with the opposite sex may be formed for many of the same reasons.

The students in these schools seem to have more maturity and self-confidence in dealing with sexuality than many adults are willing to credit them with. This suggests that one thing the schools could do to help students is to treat them as unique individuals and respect the thought that has gone into their attitudes toward sex. It would be well if the schools could also provide someone the students could talk to freely, honestly, and with confidence. Without this essential ingredient, the schools' efforts in sex education or sex counseling will probably come to naught. But this means that the schools must take their students' sexuality seriously, and that they must show their students the same kind of respect they would like their students to show them.

Minorities in Independent Schools

In some circles the elite independent schools have a reputation as bastions of WASP society and there has probably been some truth in this view in the past (see McLachlan, 1970). Although many of the elite schools have welcomed minority students from their founding, others have not been so open. Furthermore, in the past, the religious requirements of the schools, combined with their cost made the schools unattractive and inaccessible to poor, black, Jewish, and Catholic students. The costs of the schools were barriers to each succeeding wave of immigrants. However, the numbers of Irish, Poles, Jews, and finally, blacks, have increased in the schools over the last century, as families in each of these groups were better able to afford the tuition, and as the schools took their religious requirements less seriously.

Particularly, more and more black students have attended the elite schools in recent years, although they are still a small minority at most schools. A very few schools are still all white, but most have some black students and some have fairly large numbers of black students. Contrary to the image of the elite schools as protective enclaves of an exclusively white society, the schools have actively sought black and other minority students. The recruiting efforts seem to have had some success, considering the obstacles of the high tuitions, boarding requirements, and rural locations of many of the schools. This section is not concerned with the recruiting efforts, however. It is concerned with what happens to black students when they get to the independent schools and with black students' reactions to their experience. We have concentrated on black students because of their significance for the schools. Since there were only 104 black students in our study, we will not report their questionnaire results in detail, but will instead attempt to provide a general portrait, based on the most salient findings.

Many of the black students in the elite schools are there on scholarships or special programs like ABC. (ABC stands for A Better Chance, Independent School Talent Search, a program which provides scholarships to disadvantaged students. Over 80 percent of the ABC students are black, the rest are a mixture of other minority students and poor white. To 1970, participating schools had contributed over $6 million in scholarships. Additional funds come from corporations and foundations.) Our results indicate that on the average black students come from much less wealthy and less highly educated families than the typical white elite school student. There are exceptions, of course, but the black student whose parents have as much money as the typical white parent is very rare. However, the black students have high educational aspirations; in fact, a higher percentage of blacks planned to attain advanced degrees than whites.

This corresponds to many surveys of black college applicants and black college students which have shown a similar high level of academic aspiration (e.g., Bayer and Boruch, 1969; Baird et al., 1973). The general long-term life goals of black students were also basically the same as those of whites: personal happiness, a happy family life, and understanding other people. Few black or white students were interested in a life involving political leadership or artistic creation. Independent school black students put slightly more value on changing the world for the better and living one's life in one's own way. Blacks and whites also seemed to have similar feelings about relations with the opposite sex. Both groups were dissatisfied with opportunities for meeting and associating with members of the opposite sex, but blacks were even more dissatisfied than whites. Blacks were especially dissatisfied with the opportunities in the local communities, and in extracurricular activities. The lack of potential black girlfriends or boyfriends at the schools causes many black students to travel home on weekends. The separation from the school adds to the blacks' sense of isolation when they return. Many black students commented on the difficulties of dating and interpersonal relations at their schools. The comments suggest that these difficulties are a major source of dissatisfaction for black students.

Most other differences were fairly small, although they were intriguing. For example, blacks were as satisfied with the extracurricular activities per se but did not participate as much as whites. Blacks were less satisfied with the amount and quality of free time at their schools, and perceived less provision for privacy than did whites. They agreed on the qualities that make for student leadership. Black students were as unhappy with the rules as whites, and were even more unhappy about restrictions on free movement. Blacks and whites were equally satisfied with the counseling, but more blacks than whites felt that the counseling intended to help students adjust to the school was inadequate. Blacks and whites generally agreed on the basis for grading, but the blacks apparently had more confidence in the objectivity and fairness of grading.

The results for several questions suggested that black students often feel alone in the elite school world. One indication was their assessment of the quality of communication between individuals and groups in their schools. They felt that teachers communicate reasonably well with individual students, but poorly with student groups. As might be predicted, blacks gave a considerably lower rating than did whites to the quality of communication between students of different races. But they also gave a lower rating to the quality of communications between individual students and other individual students. Perhaps black students on many campuses feel they can talk freely with very few other students. They may feel that other students do not understand their feelings when they do talk, or that they are seen as stereotypes rather than individuals.

Another indication came in the responses of blacks to the question about whom they would turn to if faced with problems in various areas. Whereas the whites consistently mentioned other students as a source of advice and help, the blacks did so much less often.

Overall, blacks felt they had gained less from their elite school experiences than did their white counterparts. The pattern was much the same, however. Blacks, like whites, felt they had made little progress toward any vocational skill, but had made progress toward a keener ability to think and an improved sense of responsibility. Blacks also felt the schools had helped them learn to understand those who differed from themselves in racial background, and had improved their ability to work with people who differed from themselves in other ways. The experience of living in a school engulfed by students of another race should lead to some accommodation and understanding. Blacks felt less help from the schools than did whites in increasing their desire to learn, their ability to stick to a task, their psychological independence from their parents, and their ability to make ethical or moral distinctions.

Black students in some elite schools have prepared brochures describing their experiences for the benefit of prospective black students. In general, these descriptions seem to have a common theme: "If you want a first rate academic education, this is a good school to get it, but be aware that you will be isolated, and will probably feel quite alone in the sea of whites, although the union of black students may provide some help." The descriptions go on to give specific instances of this theme which apply to each school. Black students are frequently made to feel they "represent" all blacks, and they are not seen as individuals in their own right. Other black students feel they cannot relate to the rich WASP lifestyles of white students.

Let us now turn to the relations among black and white students per se. In order to gain information about racial and ethnic relations at the elite independent schools, the people in this study were asked to check the three phrases from a list of thirteen that were most generally true at their school. The phrases most often chosen by students were, ' Treat each other as individuals rather than as members of groups" (chosen by 46 percent), "Treat each other fairly" (41 percent), "Like each other" (33 percent), and "Learn from each other" (31 percent). Teachers and administrators also chose the first two phrases above, but their third choice was "Try to understand each other's problems."

Comments tended to present the same picture that is shown in the questionnaire responses. For example, many persons explained that their school had few minority group members. "Our school, unfortunately, is lilywhite and European." Others pointed to the consequences of this fact: "There are very few members of other ethnic groups and as a result a minority group sticks together though superficial friendliness is apparent but how deep the friendliness goes—I don't know." Some said there was an unrecognized bias.

In spite of the amiability between people of all races at this school, I think most of the students here, as is the case with most of America, are unconsciously racist, feeling that the white anglo-saxon culture is superior. Thus this produces a kind of patronizing condescension on the part of many of the students.

Some whites felt that black students were not perfect.

There are some blacks as lousy as some lousy whites.

It is the Negroes who are considered under the category of race relations (with whites.)—Other relations are so relaxed they are not worth mentioning. At this school, the Negroes, with the help of the Afro-American Society, move apart from the others *in general* (not in all cases) and in all 4 classes. They seem to feel they need a unity that is more than racial history, even trying to gain permission to live together in their own dormitory—I am a WASP, and view from the outside, but I consider myself impartial on race; it is the exclusive grouping that annoys me, and it seems like racism and segregationism in full color. The Negroes this month have entirely declined interest in campus unrest, involved only with the problems of their own race and their militant heroes. . . . The whites seem more willing to be friendly . . .

But many individuals felt that when differences are recognized, they can be the basis of greater understanding and cooperation: "We are beginning to realize that there are definite differences and are beginning to talk them out, and trying to learn together."

Items from other areas suggest that students are greatly concerned about racial and ethnic relations (presumably on a national basis) and would like to see their school provide courses about race relations.

What the Schools Have Done for Minorities

As noted earlier, the ABC (A Better Chance) program has actively sought out talented minority students from poor families for the independent schools. About 80 percent of the ABC students have been black. Most of the money has come from the schools themselves, although federal and philanthropic funds have sometimes helped the program considerably. The program has provided many black students with the means to attend one of the elite schools. In addition, some long established independent schools have always welcomed black students—schools such as Andover, Exeter, Northfield-Mt. Hermon, and Wooster, among others. Although the schools have been able to give scholarships to minority students for a number of years, they may have to curtail these programs in the future as their finances become tighter.

Whether there will be more or fewer black students in independent schools, the problems of adaptation for both the white schools and the black students will probably remain. The schools continue to have a strong upper middle or upper class orientation that may be difficult for many black students to accept. The rural isolation of some schools may also bother some black students. White stereotypes and ignorance about blacks are yet other causes for concern. The schools may be understandably reluctant to attempt to deal with these concerns, since they must enter new and unfamiliar areas. As Kraushaar (1972) has pointed out "Encounters with young people whose emotional and intellectual needs vary strikingly from those of the usual run of white middle and upper class students call for forays into the untried and unknown: new and different remedial work and counseling, special studies, unprecedented social and disciplinary problems, and the unpleasant task of placating loud-talking constituents who if not wholly antagonistic to such experiments are chary of them." In the absence of such efforts (and sometimes even with their presence), the black students in many schools have turned to each other for social, moral, and emotional support. Black unions, student associations, and leagues have sprung up on many campuses. In most cases the organizations exist to help black students cope with demands of their schools, but in some schools the organizations have been dominated by militants who favor belligerency and separatism. In a few instances, there has been a corresponding belligerent response on the part of the administration, and some tense situations have been the result. However, as the schools and blacks have gained more experience dealing with each other, some patterns of accommodation and respect seem to have developed. The results of the programs and informal efforts at some schools indicate that black students can add to the educational and personal experiences the schools provide for their students. The key may be to avoid trying to "integrate" black students by attempting to get them to become like everyone else but rather to accept and capitalize on their perspectives and contributions to school life.

The experiences of blacks in independent schools suggest that many other students, who are unlike the white, Protestant middle class, academically-oriented youth who comprise the bulk of the students, may have similar reactions. The schools may have a somewhat different impact on students who come from low income families, inner city homes, or non-WASP ethnic groups. For example, research at the college level has shown that students bring their homes, peers, and communities with them when they enter a new educational situation. The general degree of compatibility of these background factors with the new educational experience can have a powerful effect on students' satisfaction and educational growth.

Students from working or lower middle class homes, from many ethnic backgrounds or from rural backgrounds often have had less stimulating intellectual and cultural experiences than most independent school students. As summarized by Feldman and Newcomb (1969), students of lower socioeconomic status, compared to their higher status counterparts: (1) are less culturally sophisticated; (2) have had a more restricted range of experiences; and (3) are more likely to be oriented to education in terms of vocational or professional training and less likely to be oriented in terms of intellectual growth. Some low status students probably have come from homes and schools that hampered rather than aided their academic growth, and these experiences affect their approach to education. At the college level, these educational differences have been found to be related to adjustment in college in several studies.

Feldman and Newcomb (1969) have suggested an "incongruity" hypothesis about the overall relation of background to college impact which may be applicable to the elite schools. They hypothesize that "... the college will have the greatest impact on entering students whose orientations are incongruent with the dominant orientation of the college. By the same token, change will be greater among students whose previous environment is discontinuous with that of the college than among those whose environment is continuous." After examining a variety of studies with different designs, purposes, measures, and results they concluded that the influence of background is complex.

Our best guess at the moment is that a college is most likely to have the largest impact on students who experience a continuing series of not-too-threatening discontinuities. Too great a divergence between student and college, especially initially, may result in the marshalling of resistances. Too little might mean no impetus for change. From this point of view, a college's objectives might include that of inculcating a tolerance, or even a desire, for those discrepancies that can stimulate change and growth (p. 332).

Feldman and Newcomb's working hypothesis, along with other results on cultural sophistication, suggest a number of possible courses of action for the independent schools. They might assign special advisors to students moderately incongruent with the school's environment. Knowledge of the intellectual and cultural backgrounds of students could help instructors choose teaching strategies that would result in the maximal growth of their students. With the same knowledge, schools could organize extracurricular programs that would offer a variety of educational experiences to aid students' development. Counseling programs could use knowledge of students' backgrounds as one basis for understanding students' problems in adjusting to school.

All of this may seem to have taken us rather far afield from the situation of minority students in independent schools. However, the research and suggestions just outlined are relevant to minorities by the general rule they suggest: the school may have its greatest impact on students who are a moderate distance from the norm of the school, and that the school may have to make a considerable effort to have an impact on students who are a large distance from the norm of the school. Although most minority students will be very similar to other elite school students, some will be very different from the typical student. To provide a high quality of education to all their students, the schools need to recognize these differences and develop the best educational program for each student.

Conclusions

Let us consider the elite school experience from the student's point of view. As a child grows up he spends the first years with his family and his neighborhood friends. The family and friends form a special and protective world. When he goes to elementary school, he usually finds many of the same friends and other children from the neighborhood who also become friends and acquaintances. He usually spends the entire day with his classmates and a single teacher. After school he returns to his family and his friends of the immediate neighborhood. The child has a place and an identity at home, in school, and with his friends. Then at about the beginning of one of the most stressful periods of his life, puberty, the child is sent away from home and friends to one of the elite schools. Here, instead of the friends he has grown up with, he faces strangers; instead of his family he faces a group of adults he has never met before; instead of a single teacher, he must deal with a succession of teachers; instead of a place and a secure sense of himself, he has an ill-defined and discontinuous identity. The reputation he may have had, for example, as being good at sports or in class or in games, must now be made anew. There is no single adult he can relate to from situation to situation. He is thrown into continuous interaction with other students in class, in required sports, at meals, in study hall, and in his house or dormitory. It then becomes essential for him to establish a stable and supportive relationship with other students. Given these conditions, he almost certainly will try to restructure as much of the kind of relations he had with his family and friends in elementary school (Turner, 1964).

It is easy to see, then, why students would value friendliness, openness, and pleasing personalities more than anything else. Friendly, pleasing fellow students make the reconstruction of the student's sense of the early years much easier. To establish a secure, stable sense of himself, the student turns to other students. Students faced with a new, strange, and somewhat impersonal environment also seek regard, approval, and affection from other students. Of course, other students wrapped up in their own needs cannot completely replace the family and the home community; neither can the adults in the school. As one girl said "Somehow students will have to be comforted the first year. They will not go to friends when they are homesick unless they feel like almost dying. *I do.* In other words we sort of need privacy or *help.*" But other students are almost the only people a student can turn to for approval from others, and, subsequently, for self-regard. And, eventually students do find stable friends and develop secure relationships with their roommates, housemates and classmates. These friends not only provide friendship but give each other support and help each other survive psychologically. The student community is frequently much more understanding of students than the professional adults.

Groups of students also can create ways to respond to the pressures of school life which stem from school rules and restrictions, classwork, difficult adults, etc. Student groups seem to smooth the transition from home to school, and to help students adapt to school life. They appear to be successful. For example, in any group of entering ninth graders there will be some small, shy twelve year olds who still have a little "baby fat." One's reaction is to think "What are those little children doing here? They should be home with their mothers and fathers." When one compares these students with their confident and resourceful senior counterparts one must credit much of the change to the students themselves. Finally, of course, other students are sources of plain fun and good times. Any institution that concentrates on particular goals as strongly as the elite schools concentrate on academic preparation needs to have an underside that allows horseplay, laughter, and enjoyment. The national youth culture can give students enjoyable experiences and provide a way for students to enjoy each other. The special interests of youth acquire special value as a focus for their relations with one another, and these interests help them distinguish themselves from the surrounding adult school world. In sum, student groups help the students in them to adapt to the school, to each other, and to themselves. Without the student groups, the schools probably would not be viable.

4
The Teachers, Teaching, and Programs of the Schools

The first part of this chapter describes the backgrounds, experience and complex roles of the teachers and administrators in the schools. The next section discusses the difficult tasks teachers face in and out of the classroom, as well as the behaviors of teachers when they are teaching their classes. The following section provides an account of extracurricular activities, an important source of satisfaction to many students. The concluding section describes the schools' efforts to provide counseling and guidance for students.

The Roles of the Teachers and Administrators

In many ways the roles of teachers and administrators in independent schools are similar to the roles of their counterparts in public schools. Teachers face many of the same joys and frustrations of working with students, the weight of day-to-day routine, and the problems of dealing with the administrative head of the school. However, the intensity and engulfing nature of the elite school environments affect the teachers and administrators as well as the students, and produce an atmosphere different from the public schools. The small size of the schools, and the intimacy and closeness of all the people in the schools means that everyone is in fairly direct contact with each other most of the time. Teachers and administrators are also often required to take on many extra duties such as coaching, leading extracurricular activities, serving as housemasters, and working on many committees. The days are long. In such close circumstances, there is little need for the formalities and bureaucracy so much a part of many public schools. Because of the closeness of the schools, everyone is more personally accountable for his or her work than in many public schools. Teachers and administrators are also much more likely to be judged on merit rather than seniority or academic credits. Of course, the schools also expect a considerable commitment from their teachers and administrators. Kraushaar has described the life of the independent school teacher, which contrasts sharply with the bureaucratic, prescribed role of the public school teacher:

The private school teacher's world is very different. He is more likely to be working in a small, unitary school run by a headmaster or principal who as a rule enjoys a generous delegation of authority by his governing board, to which he is solely accountable. He is the captain of the ship. Relationships within the school tend to be informal and familial, and the teacher is allowed considerable leeway in what and how he teaches. The private school teacher is generally poorly paid, sometimes way below his public school colleague. Yet his salary level, such as it is, is more likely to reflect both experience and merit; and he may be asked to assume part-time administrative duties while still remaining, in fact and in spirit, a member of the faculty. If he works in a boarding school, his duties are likely to be multiple, including housemastering and coaching, and his day a long one. The day school teacher too, in addition to teaching a variety of subjects each requiring separate preparation, is likely to be called on to take on a spate of extracurricular duties such as athletic coaching and directing other activities. . . .

The profile of the independent school teacher, emerging out of a welter of individual differences, is that of the dedicated amateur—a man or woman broadly educated in the humanistic liberal arts tradition, not highly specialized, and but lightly burdened, if at all, with the pedagogical formalism of professional education. More than likely he is of Protestant background (Episcopal, Presbyterian, or Congregational), wears his religion lightly, but believes firmly in the importance of character education. At the same time, since he is aware of the youth counter-culture, he is less certain now just how the development of character is to be accomplished. And even if his background is Catholic or Jewish—and their number is increasing—he tends to accept the traditional WASP moral and social standards, though perhaps with growing doubts. Whatever the ethnic origin or religious loyalties of the independent school teacher, he is uncomfortably aware that the assimilation of students of heterogeneous origins to the old Anglo-Saxon standards is not working as it once did, except possibly in a few of the prestigious bastions of meritocracy concentrated in New England and in scattered replications elsewhere, particularly in the South. And even there, the old confidence and self-assurance are being eroded by the young radicals with their insistent questioning of authority, assumption of eccentric life-styles, and the spreading drug culture (pp. 144-145).

The academic life of the elite school teacher is unusual in many other ways. First his or her classes are typically quite small, usually no larger than fifteen students. This situation may sound ideal, but there are many classes, and students require a great deal of individual attention from teachers, thus demanding great effort and time from teachers. The students often require time from teachers outside of class too; the best teachers are often sought as counselors, organizers, or sponsors of activities, or just someone to talk to. As one teacher told me, "Students think you have all the time in the world to talk with them and go through the same vague watery ideas you have heard a hundred times. They will leave you with no life of your own." Some schools, such as the Hebron Academy, frankly state that ". . . faculty . . . are selected not only for their academic qualifications, but also for their enthusiasm and for their willingness to devote an enormous amount of non-class time to working with young people." (*Independent Secondary Schools: A Handbook.*) The reasons teachers and administrators choose to work and live in this intense environment are described later in this chapter.

Salaries and Other Benefits

Considering the affluence of the students' families, the high tuition, and the size of the endowments, one might expect the teachers to be well paid. This is not the case. National Association of Independent Schools figures showed that the average salary in boys' boarding schools in 1975-1976 was $8,850; the typical figures ranging between $7,500 and $10,400, although single salaries as low as $4,000 and as high as $24,000 were reported. In most schools the salaries seldom went higher than $18,000. The median salary in boys' day schools was $10,900. In girls' boarding schools the average salary was $8,300; the typical salaries ranging between $7,500 and $9,000, with a range of salaries as low as $4,000 and as high as $15,200. The median salary in girls' day schools was $9,200. (The comparable national average for public high school teachers was approximately $12,500.) Of course, these figures do not include some financial benefits that are provided for teachers in many schools, particularly the boarding schools. A number of schools provide faculty housing at a nominal cost. In addition, many of the boarding schools use a house system in which faculty members and their families live in houses with students. The faculty families usually have several rooms or an apartment in the house. The rest of the house is divided into student rooms and study rooms or lounges. The house system is a mixed blessing for the faculty families, however. They must give a great deal of their time to counseling, disciplining, and simply talking to students. There is little time that is really private. In many of the boarding schools, faculty families share meals with the students in the dining hall. Again, this provides financial advantages, but at the price of privacy and personal choice. Finally, the schools encourage husband-wife teams, so that some families have two incomes from the school.

The teachers are generally well educated—33 percent have a bachelor's degree, 59 percent have a master's, and 5 percent have a doctorate. The comparative figures for public secondary school teachers are 64 percent with bachelor's, 34 percent with master's, and 1 percent with doctorates. The schools list the colleges from which their staff received degrees; most lists are fairly impressive, often including foreign institutions. Elite school teachers were also experienced. Half had been teaching ten or more years, nearly a quarter more than twenty years. Among public high school teachers about 40 percent have been teaching ten or more years, and 14 percent had been teaching for twenty or more years.

If elite school teachers are somewhat better educated and more experienced than their public school colleagues, yet are paid less—between $2,000 and $4,000 less on the average—why do they come to the independent schools, and why do they stay? One clue is found in the kinds of secondary schools the teachers attended. Some 40 percent had attended independent schools. (Eighty-five percent of the public school teachers had attended public schools.) Thus, many independent school teachers seem attracted to an educational setting they had experienced themselves, and which they presumably found satisfying. Another clue lies in the teachers' educational backgrounds. Most independent school teachers majored in the liberal arts and sciences during college—mathematics, English, history, languages, etc.—rather than in education. This fact suggests that most independent school teachers may not have intended to become teachers when they entered college, but that they saw teaching in the independent schools as a way to keep up with their fields and pass on their interests and knowledge to bright young minds. Of course, they may have had difficulty finding other employment, or they may have lacked teaching credentials which would have prevented their entry into public schools. However, there are many reasons to believe that the main reasons teachers choose independent schools are academic rather than economic. For example, Kraushaar (1972) found additional reasons when he asked teachers why they chose to teach in independent schools. The most important reasons for the teachers' decisions to go to independent schools were the freedom to design and teach courses as they wished, the lower student-teacher ratio, the freedom they felt to teach their classes in their own way, their feeling of being part of a personal community, their respect for the school head, their regard for the quality of other teachers and the students, the particular educational philosophy of their schools, and the opportunity the schools provide for study and thorough class preparation. These reasons seem to reflect a need for academic autonomy and the desire to work in an intellectually stimulating environment. It seems that teachers, like students, choose elite schools primarily for academic reasons.

The Administrators

Administrators are very similar to the teachers just described, logically enough, because most are recruited from the ranks of the teachers. They held about as many degrees as the teachers, but had been at their schools for more years, had been teaching for more years (62 percent had been teaching for ten or more years) and, of course, were older (forty-three compared to thirty-eight years of age). One interesting fact is that about half had attended independent schools themselves compared to 40 percent of the teachers. The similarity between teachers and administrators should cause no surprise, since most "administrators" in independent schools also teach. When we asked respondents to choose the phrase that best described their role in the school, over twice as many chose "teacher-administrator" as chose "administrator." It is quite common for an admissions officer, dean of faculty, or assistant to the headmaster to be an instructor in English, mathematics, or history.

In most of these schools the teacher-administrators individually have much less prestige and power than the headmaster. The headmasters are the centers of school life in most schools. They are not the autonomous commanders-in-chief they once were, but even today they play a crucial role in the schools as the ultimate resting place of legitimate power. As Seymour Sarason has pointed out in his perceptive book on *The Culture of the School and the Problem of Change*, it is usually difficult to accomplish anything in a school without the permission of the school head, and it is virtually impossible to carry through a major change without the head's active support. The head now needs to work through committees, assistants, boards, and advisors, but he or she is still by far the most important person in the school.

The administration of the independent schools, whether in the role of headmaster or teacher-administrator is a complex and difficult task. Although the schools retain their good academic reputations, which, in turn, draw parental support, the problems of rising operating costs, faculty demands, racial equality, and public expectations present difficult and continuous problems. An administrator, particularly the headmaster, must satisfy many groups. As Robert Hutchins (paraphrased by Otto Kraushaar) points out, an administrator ". . . deals with at least six constituencies: the faculty, the trustees, the students, the parents, the alumni, and the public, each of which could claim much of his time. And there is always the hazard . . . that he will spend just enough time with each of the six to irritate the other five."

It is hard for a teacher to learn how to be an administrator. Apparently there are no established moves nor established channels to be followed in order to reach the top position in the schools. There are few programs to train independent school administrators, either in-service programs or academic programs in universities. This is in sharp contrast to the formalized pathways in public schools. The usual—if there is a usual—pattern is for a teacher to be asked to head a committee to deal with some administrative problem, then to be asked to take over some "administrative" task, such as helping in admissions work. Then, if the teacher does these jobs well, he or she might assume some formal title, such as dean of students. After a few years in this position, if our new dean has worked successfully with teachers, administrators, and trustees, he or she might be seen as headmaster material. Then, assuming that the previous head retires or finds another job, the dean might be considered for the head position. Another possibility is that, in the relatively small world of the elite schools, another school will have heard of the good person, and consider him or her for their head. Whatever the route, it seems as determined by chance and luck as by ability and skill. Administrative skill, difficult to evaluate in the best of circumstances, also seems to take a back seat to moral and "leadership" qualities when trustees select a new head, according to Karushaar's results. Thus, it is little wonder that the new head assumes his or her new position with only a haphazard prepartion for the position.

The work of the head then becomes that of leading the school, which means that the head must deal with teachers, other administrators, students, and the mundane details of garbage collection, food services, books and supplies, athletic equipment, student discipline problems, and keeping the school out of financial trouble. These multitudinous and multifaceted problems have been well described by Kraushaar, and are beyond our immediate purposes. Kraushaar also described a general problem that seems to override the problems of finance and administration, which may be behind many of the other problems:

The traditional model that young people in independent schools were expected to emulate was the WASP gentleman: the versatile, clean-cut well-mannered, prudent man of affairs, who, favored by the circumstances of his birth, plans his life and invests his time and money carefully with the goal of becoming rich, respected, and influential—a pillar of society. It was the ideal of the ruling class that set the tone and standard of success in American politics, business and industry, society, education, and the professions from colonial times until well into the twentieth century. It is also the ideal that a growing segment of young people, including those who are to the manor born, are questioning vigorously today. The fact that this life-style is being viewed with growing misgivings or outright disdain (and in some cases flatly rejected) by some of the brightest and most advantaged students deeply troubles their parents and perplexes the headmasters of the prestigious schools, most particularly the boys' boarding schools. They sense that their traditional mission—forwarding their graduates to the Ivy League colleges—is in danger of losing its validity, while there is no clear vision of a fresh goal that is viable under the existing pattern of private school support (pp. 180-181).

The next section details the way teachers have attempted to meet this, as well as more traditional challenges.

Teachers and Teaching

Many of the demands placed on independent school teachers are like those placed on teachers everywhere. Good teaching does not come "naturally," even to the person with a knack for it. For example, although most people can participate in a group conversation, the effective teacher needs to know how to lead discussions so that more than the usual eager few have a chance to express their views. The teacher also needs to know when to be silent. After years of experience in receiving grades, new teachers feel familiar with the grading process, but when they have to do the grading themselves, they realize how complicated it can be. They need to decide whether students' levels of effort or achievement are more important, and need to work out ways for the grades they give to take into account the differences in students' ability, speed, and persistence. Teachers need to award their grades constructively, so that students can see what they have done correctly or incorrectly and can see how they can change to improve their performance. Independent school teachers especially need to find ways to motivate the bright but lazy or uninterested student. There are pragmatic problems as well, that bear especially heavily on independent schools, for example, making good use of difficult times in the schedule, such as Friday afternoons, days before holidays, and the last class of the day.

Like their public school counterparts, independent school teachers need to have some kind of program to develop their students' ability to inquire, to discover, and to think critically. The program needs to be different in various fields, of course, but sensitive teachers need practice and models to follow before they can work out the program that seems personally best to them. This may involve the development of challenging class projects, the invention of games, using students as tutors, writing creative class exercises, or team learning, as well as the more common methods. One problem which bears especially on independent school teachers is to find ways to make the rather traditional content of their courses personally significant to students. Because of the rather narrow range of social backgrounds of the students, independent school teachers sometimes need to help students become less bound to their backgrounds and usual manner of thinking about things so they can see events and ideas in a broader social context. Finally, teachers in boarding schools often have to make special efforts to help students develop their sense of themselves and gain a sound sense of self-respect so that they can adapt to the boarding situation.

The classroom tasks just outlined are only part of the role of the independent school teacher. For many teachers, the most difficult problems arise when they must cope with students' parents. They may encounter parents who do not really understand teaching in many ways. For example, some parents may feel that learning goes on only when a student is studying, or that such subjects as English should consist of grammar lessons, not discussing contemporary problems, reading "controversial" books, or thinking critically. Other parents feel that only a good disciplinarian and lecturer is a good teacher. Some may take the credit for their children's successes, but blame the teacher for their children's failures. Teachers, particularly in boarding schools, may have to deal with parents who shirk their responsibilities. These parents force teachers to teach students things they should learn at home, including common manners and ordinary morality. They may expect the teachers and the schools to raise their children for them, and do, in a short period, what they, the parents, have not done in fourteen years. Other parents have set ideas about teaching and values, and may object to innovations. They may feel that teachers somehow *make* students learn, rather than helping students learn. Some parents of independent school students believe strongly in competition, class rank, grades, and exact knowledge of hard facts, thus resenting teaching innovations. Other parents may have their children's lives mapped out and therefore feel that a low grade will disrupt their plans. Some parents cannot accurately gauge the abilities of their children and pressure the students too hard for unrealistically high grades or academic achievement. Some independent school parents with advanced degrees feel their children must follow in their footsteps, even when they do not have the ability. They may make children miserable when they do not get A's. Other parents may want independent school teachers to be low-payed saints who have perfect families, wear conservative clothes, and smile through it all.

Students also have expectations regarding their teachers' behavior. Research has suggested that new students expect their teachers to be stimulating, engaging, vital, and friendly (Pace, 1966). By the time they become seniors, they lower their expectations considerably, but they still expect their teachers to be reasonably well organized, well informed about their subject, reasonable in their demands for work, and fair in grading. If a teacher does not meet these minimal expectations, students are likely to be dissatisfied and may complain. In the next section, we study the ways students assess their teachers' performance in comparison to their expectations.

Teaching Practices

The characteristic ways in which instructors teach their classes can have important consequences for their students' learning, satisfaction, and development. For example, a history teacher could emphasize technical knowledge of her subject, be concerned with the effects of the knowledge of history in the personal development of her students, or attempt to make her students think like scholars. The way in which she teaches her course helps determine what her students get out of it. Her teaching style reflects her values and the goals she hopes her students will attain.

There have been many attempts to describe the teaching behaviors of instructors by such varied methods as systematic observation, rating methods, and measures of social interaction. Recently there have been a number of attempts to describe the classroom environment by surveys asking students about classroom procedures and qualities. The latter approach seems to offer the advantage that students describe what has occurred to them as they perceive it, and indicate whether it was a characteristic part of their classroom experience. The assumption behind this approach is that the perceptions of students, the persons most affected by teaching styles, are useful descriptions of what goes on in the classroom. (The perceptions of teachers offer a valuable comparison to student perceptions.) It is teacher behavior as it is *received* and interpreted; in the case of teachers it is behavior as it is *sent*, or intended. Of course, we cannot ask students and teachers about everything they may have experienced or done. Classroom experiences vary greatly, and what is important to one student or teacher may not be so to another. We therefore attempted to isolate the features of classroom teaching that are important for the majority of students and teachers.

Consequently, we developed a question based on the major aspects of classroom teaching which had been identified in previous studies and the experiences of groups of teachers. Although there appears to be a bewildering diversity among these studies and experiences, a careful review of them indicated some degree of consensus. From this review and from an intuitive analysis of teacher behaviors that are visible in typical school classes, a number of items dealing with teacher-student interaction were developed. The items are descriptions of teachers' behaviors, rather than evaluations of behavior.

The overall results for these items, shown in Table 4-1, indicate that 70 percent of students, teachers, and administrators thought that the majority of teachers "give friendly help to any student having problems with school work," "try to be sure that students understand the work that is done in class," "are very friendly toward their students outside of class," "encourage classroom discussion," and "cover a great deal of material in the time allowed for the course." The three least characteristic traits presented a description as follows: most teachers do not "try to make their classes entertaining rather than useful," do not "involve students in the choice of class goals and classroom procedures," and do not "place too much emphasis on detailed facts and memorization."

These items suggest that most teachers are careful in organizing their classwork while avoiding deadening detail and are friendly to their students, although they do not include them in decisions about classroom procedures.

Although teachers were described in fairly similar terms in all the schools, the students, teachers, and administrators in the schools did not agree on every item. For seven items, the majority of teachers and administrators felt that the item was true of many or most teachers, while the majority of students felt it was true of very few or only some teachers. Three of these items deal with encouragement of originality. Students tended to feel that most teachers did not encourage students to do independent work, did not encourage originality in classwork and tests, and did not stimulate students to think and be creative; teachers and administrators tended to feel that they did all three things. Perhaps students and teachers had different things in mind when they considered independent work and creativity. For example, to some teachers, independent work may mean providing a choice of additional books that can be read for credit, but to students such books may be just another part of standard classwork.

In these times it is no surprise that students also tended to think that teachers did not make their class material relevant to current trends and events, while teachers felt that they did. And it is no surprise that students felt that teachers did not make their courses interesting while teachers felt they did. But it may surprise independent school teachers who feel they work intensively with students and have rigorous standards, that many students felt that most teachers are not understanding of students' academic problems and do not push students to the limits of the students' abilities. The first result seems contradictory with

Table 4-1

Teaching Practices of Independent School Teachers

(in percentages)

	Group					
	Students		Teachers		Administrators	
Item	F-S*	M	F-S	M	F-S	M
Teachers clearly outline and organize their courses	30	67	18	70	17	72
Teachers encourage classroom discussion	25	74	14	83	11	82
Teachers try to make the class material relevant to current trends and events	55	44	28	67	36	56
Teachers involve students in the choice of class goals and classroom procedures	74	21	72	18	61	26
Teachers give friendly help to any student having problems with classwork	16	83	7	91	5	93
Teachers try to be sure that students understand the work that is done in class	22	76	6	89	4	84
Teachers cover a great deal of material in the time allowed for the course	19	77	9	77	15	69
Teachers place too much emphasis on detailed facts and memorization	66	30	67	20	67	17
Teachers give students a broad general understanding of the subject	36	59	17	74	15	73
Teachers push students to the limits of the students' abilities	58	37	41	52	35	58
Teachers encourage students to do independent work	59	38	47	49	39	56
Teachers are understanding of students' academic problems	49	47	18	77	16	77
Teachers stimulate students to think and be creative	57	39	40	57	27	66
Teachers succeed in making their courses interesting to students	62	35	33	60	31	61
Teachers try to make their classes entertaining rather than useful	89	5	85	5	86	2
Teachers encourage originality in classwork and tests	60	36	36	56	37	52
Teachers are clear about what they expect in assignments and tests	24	73	8	84	8	79
Teachers are very friendly toward their students outside of class	23	75	14	84	8	86

Source: *Questionnaire for Students, Teachers and Administrators* and *Questionnaire for New Students,* Educational Testing Service and the Secondary School Research Program, © 1971, 1972, Educational Testing Service.

*F-S = Characteristic of "Very Few" or "some"; M = Characteristic of "Many" or "Most"

The item read as follows: Please indicate how characteristic or true each statement is of the teachers at your school.

the result that most teachers give friendly help to any student having difficulty with classwork. But "academic problems" are broader than difficulty with classwork. They may include personal difficulties with certain subjects, getting a lower grade than the student thinks he or she deserves, etc. The second result may be due to students' feelings that they have something in reserve that they can call on, or that most classes do not really involve all their abilities.

Many students and teachers commented about teaching in the elite schools. Some were concerned about particular points. Others commented on the complexities of teaching. For example, a teacher commented:

I am one of those teachers who tends to point out all the errors, on the assumption that a good or right answer is its own reward. It may be interesting to see just where the positive reinforcements come in in any given situation—from the student and teacher points of view. For example, vocal praise for good work may be considered by a teacher as a positive reinforcement—but may be considered embarrassing, insincere and therefore worthless, stated to bolster the teacher's ego, resented as attention by an authority figure—etc.

And a student thought that all "teachers stimulate some students—even terrible teachers stimulate *somebody*."

A few students felt that teachers really do not care about their students:

I personally have no teachers who involve students in the choice of class goals and especially classroom procedures. Teachers may involve their students in a project but there is no choice of goals or procedures. There should be some type of teacher evaluation. Also, none of my teachers are "friendly." Most have the attitude of "I don't care about you," "you come to me and ask for help and I'll give it." But as to an individual, they never offer aid. They don't care if you understand; they don't give a broad understanding of the subject, teachers aren't understanding of students' academic problems, there is no creative stimulation, courses are boring and a waste of time; no originality whatsoever in tests especially and classwork; teachers are generally hostile and defensive of their students because the students refuse to pay back the respect that the teachers demand.

In contrast, some students praised their teachers:

The teachers are what make this school. I am at a boarding school and the teachers are readily available to students at any time for discussion of assignments or classwork or just general discussion and relief from pressures of school. They're there to talk with and to relate.

Although few students were as disappointed as the student quoted earlier, some felt that classwork was boring:

A large part of the student body has at one time or another been depressed and very bored. If classes were more interesting and if teachers weren't so hard (by this I mean stressing grades and general attitude) then maybe the feeling of apathy along with depression would cease to exist.

However, as another student pointed out:

It's up to the students to make the course interesting by their attitude towards it. Some teachers *kill* the course and a student will wind up hating teacher and course despite *his attempts* to do otherwise. Some teachers want a preconceived answer to a preconceived question when there are several answers.

One common theme in student comments was that there is insufficient chance for creativity or independent thinking: "In most of the courses, the students have to repeat back to the teacher—the teacher's opinion. The student doesn't have a chance to think for himself." And "Teacher attitudes as expressed in and out of class are restrictive to originality and creative development of students generally. But students tend to be unimaginative as well. Teachers are basically out of touch, and that is the main problem—they don't really care if they're with it or not."

In response, some teachers offered their views that originality is often irrelevant to academic learning:

Some courses are of necessity limited in just how much "independent work," "creativity," and "originality" can even be included in the study of certain disciplines.

In this question, it appears that to be original is a "goal." Is it necessarily? I happen to think that graduate school is the place for originality: before that time a student cannot know whether or not he is being original; often he is just trying to be different.

Much, much, much more emphasis should be put on detailed memorization and facts; (1) memorization is an excellent discipline of the mind, and (2) the more facts one knows, the more one has to think about and the easier it is to make decisions—students depend too much on general hypothesis and theory.

Finally, there were several comments that suggest fundamental reforms of teaching based on recent theories or critiques of education. First a teacher, then a student:

Having just read Holt's *How Children Fail*, I have been noting for 2 months what may be called the fear principle operating in my classes. Maybe I found it only because I was looking for it, but it persists and continues to appall me. It seems to me that a question involving student and teacher perceptions as to the factors that motivate students to continue academic endeavors would be useful in evaluating the emotional climate in a school. Among those choices should be fear—of failure—of authority and (worst of all) a paralyzing fear of being thought ridiculous.

Although I have given my teachers a lot of credit for their efforts, I do not think these efforts are helping the student. I agree with John Holt when he says, "teachers talk too much." Dr. Maria Montessori believes that teachers (in her book, *The Montessori Method*, she is concerned with young children, but I still think this point is relevant) should be observers in a class. Teachers, in taking the primary responsibility of relating knowledge to students are defeating their purpose. People's minds work very differently from one another, and how can a teacher expect 14 other minds to think and comprehend as she does. The teacher can easily stifle the student without knowing it, confuse him horribly without need. Auto-education is the most impressive and builds a feeling of pride in self.

The Role of Grades

Grades are crucial in the interaction between teachers and students. Grades represent teachers' assessments of students and a reward for certain behaviors. Grades have an importance for students and teachers alike far beyond their importance for admission to college. To many students, grades represent evaluations not only of their performance but of their worth as persons. For these reasons, the perceptions of the importance of various factors in grading are important.

The evidence about the basis for awarding grades, student reactions to grades, and the effects of grades on students' self-conceptions is complex and voluminous (Warren, 1971). The basis for grades is certainly multidimensional and varies by subject and by instructor. However, a description of the process of grading in the schools can lead to a better understanding of the goals and values that grades serve in the elite schools.

As shown in Table 4-2, students, teachers and administrators agreed that knowledge of the subject matter, hard work, and intelligence were very important in getting good grades, and that students' family backgrounds, agreement with the teacher, and chance were relatively unimportant in getting good grades. But these results hide some real differences between the views of students and teachers and administrators. Students felt that "talking a lot in discussions," "writing fast on examinations," "chance," and "agreeing with the teacher" were much more important than did the teachers. Some 71 percent of the teachers thought "being friendly with the teacher," was unimportant in grading while 68 percent of the students thought being friendly *was* important in getting good grades. In sum, although both groups agreed that the most important factors in grades were knowledge, hard work, and intelligence, students saw much more subjectivity in grade assignments than did teachers.

Who is right? It is not sophistry to say that both groups are right, since both are reporting their evaluations of the grading process from the perspectives of their own roles. Students probably feel that other students who talk a lot in

Table 4-2
The Perceived Importance of Various Bases for Grades
(in percentages)

	Students			Teachers			Administrators		
Bases	U*	I	VI	U	I	VI	U	I	VI
Hard work	4	28	64	1	38	55	4	30	59
Good behavior in class	13	52	30	25	55	11	27	55	10
Intelligence	6	32	58	6	32	54	4	37	51
Talking a lot in discussions	5	48	43	13	62	17	8	62	21
Creativity, originality	9	42	45	3	37	51	3	28	59
Agreeing with the teacher	46	33	16	80	10	0	78	11	1
Neatness in assignments	24	58	12	28	58	6	17	66	9
Ability to write fast on examinations	32	40	22	47	39	3	35	48	5
Who a student's family is	79	9	4	91	1	0	89	0	1
Chance	45	32	8	58	21	1	61	16	2
Actual knowledge of the subject matter	4	26	66	0	10	82	0	11	81
Being friendly with the teacher	25	52	16	71	20	0	62	24	2

Source: *Questionnaire for Students, Teachers and Administrators* and *Questionnaire for New Students*, Educational Testing Service and the Secondary School Research Program, © 1971, 1972, Educational Testing Service.
*U = Unimportant; I = Of some Importance; VI = Very Important; "Can't Say" and "No Response" percentages are not shown.
The item read as follows:
Students—Please indicate how important the following *generally* are for getting good grades in *most* of your classes.
Teachers and administrators—Please indicate the *general* importance of each item for assigning good grades in the classes you teach or have taught.

class, write fast on examinations, and are friendly with the teacher do get better grades. Psychologically, some students may wish to emphasize the subjective aspects of grades, so that it is easier to live with grades below their expectations. Similarly, teachers may wish to minimize their own subjectivity in grading. To admit that one is subjective in grading could lead to painful doubts about being arbitrary and capricious.

Students' and teachers' comments about grades generally suggest the same results. Although, as one student pointed out, "most of the items mentioned are of *some* importance, they all interplay with each other. It also depends on the teacher," some students were quite dissatisfied:

I feel that my school has nearly stifled my progress in learning. Most courses stress only hard work and competition. Anyone with enough guts can get a good grade, and that's good. But it's work for the sake of exercise, and very little is actually learned. Creative thinking is stifled because it takes too long. And although the discipline is great, I am impatient to start thinking.

Others were cynical: "If you aren't friendly with a teacher you are marked a revolutionist, freak, rebel, or whatever, and promptly asked not to return." However, many students complimented their teachers:

The faculty here aren't a bunch of insecure . . . school teachers who feel they have to demand respect—rather than gain it through their own ability to express and to teach, through their honesty and openness—and through their own desire to learn themselves.

From their side, teachers admitted the difficulties in assigning grades: "It is impossible to be objective about the relationship of grades and agreeing with the teacher and friendliness. I hope that both would be unimportant, but I may be kidding myself." From the comments it appears that many teachers are concerned about the objectivity of their grading practices, and that they try to be aware of their own prejudices and try to overcome them. One conscientious teacher may be typical:

As a teacher, I cannot say what leads to good grades other than native intelligence and/or hard work. Yet, relationships with the teacher do help in the student-faculty relationship. For example: "Being friendly with the teacher" is not a reason to give a student a good grade—yet, this friendship might foster the desire on the part of the student to attain good grades. "Neatness in assignments" would never be a reason to grade a person—yet, I'm convinced, *often* results in better grades. Obviously, this whole question bothers me in its relevance for a teacher doing his or her job in an honorable way.

The teachers in independent schools seem to be conscientious and friendly. Although they try to cover a lot of material in their classes, they are careful to try to enliven the material by encouraging discussion and avoiding the dead weight of detail. The teachers clearly try to foster the academic achievement of their students, but in so doing, they may find it difficult to also foster creativity or to make the relevance of their subject plain. Most teachers take their job seriously, and try their best as human beings to do a human job, and it appears that most students respect their efforts.

The teacher in the classroom is obviously expected to perform many complex and difficult duties as part of his or her teaching role. Consider the tasks suggested in the following quotation from Feldman and Newcomb (1969: 251):

As representatives of various subject matters and disciplines, teachers can expose students—through what they say in class and through the readings they assign—to a wide variety of new knowledge, values, and ways of doing things. To some students, the teacher may be an extrinsic source of motivation pressuring the student to engage in intellectual activities and self-examinations that he might not otherwise undertake; for other students, he may support or encourage an already intrinsic motivation for learning, self-awareness, and personal growth. The teacher can be a critic, a rigorous and impartial judge of mental efforts; he can define standards of aspirations and of achievement. He can encourage a student's serious aspirations and strengthen his confidence in his own talents. He can reveal deficiencies in a student's knowledge and skills in an area and help him to correct them, or, in some cases, dissuade him from continuing in that area. The teacher may be a catalyst to the student's reorienting his value system rather completely, or he may reinforce the student's existing values and attitudes; in either case, he may press for congruence between his own values and those of his students, or he may work within the student's frame of reference and help him develop more fully his own proclivities and potentialities.

The teacher may be expected to expose students to new knowledge and skills, be a source of motivation, define standards of performance, encourage or discourage students, and serve as a modifier or supporter of values. These expectations will almost certainly vary by curriculum and type of school. Teachers in scientific fields may concentrate on knowledge; a discussion of values would be considered inappropriate. Humanities and literature courses might emphasize the discussion of values over all else. Some art courses may emphasize skills. Schools with a strongly traditional approach to religion may seek to reinforce their students' traditional outlooks, whereas some teachers in highly liberal schools may feel it their duty to call such outlooks into question. In short, much of what the teacher is expected to do in the classroom will be determined by the setting in which the teacher is imbedded.

In sum, the tasks of teaching are difficult ones; in some cases the tasks outside the classroom are more difficult than the tasks within. Students expect their teachers to do many things. The teachers judge themselves according to their own ideas of good teaching. Finally, the schools they work in have a variety of expectations for them. Some of these expectations are touched on in other chapters. We could not examine every aspect of teachers' roles, of course, although they are obviously interconnected. In this study, we decided to concentrate on the aspect of teachers' roles that is the most central to their function: their classroom teaching. In general, students seem to find their teachers to be conscientious and friendly. They also seem to respect their teachers for their competence and their concern, but harbor doubts about their concern for creativity, doubts that extend to the entire structure of the school, as we shall see throughout this book.

Extracurricular Activities and Related Aspects of the School

Although we have so far concentrated on the academic side of independent school programs, we do not wish to slight the importance of activities outside the classroom. These activities are important for several reasons. Evidence has slowly accumulated to show that extracurricular attainments are as important for aspirations and accomplishment as academic achievement (Baird, 1970; Spady, 1971). For example, the adult leaders of today often began as high school and college leaders (Matthews, 1960). Successful artists, musicians, actors, and dramatists almost always began their activities in high school and college, usually outside the classroom (Barron, 1968; Cox, 1926). Successful scientists also began an intense involvement in science in high school and college (Eiduson, 1962; Roe, 1953; Taylor and Ellison, 1967), and most successful writers began their publishing careers on high school and college newspapers, literary magazines, and annuals (Barron, 1968; MacKinnon, 1962). Some of this evidence is summarized by Baird (1976). Further evidence has also accumulated to show that students who participate in extracurricular activities are more satisfied than others with their educational careers (Berdie et al., 1970).

Of course, there is a great deal of evidence that extracurricular and academic achievements in college are predicted best by similar achievements in high school (Baird, 1976). In fact, it is rather unlikely that a student who has not been active in high school will be active in college; there are very few "latebloomers" (Baird, 1969a). In short, the best predictors of later high-level accomplishment are records of similar accomplishments. It seems logical that students who will show high-level accomplishments in college and beyond would be those students who had records of similar achievements in school.

Extracurricular activities may be especially important in independent boarding schools, where they sometimes are the only path for personal expression and escape from the intensity of academic pressure. They allow a student to be something other than Susan Jones, the B+ student; or Harvey Brown, the B− student. Students can feel a sense of accomplishment which will bolster their self-confidence and increase their willingness to tackle the academic side of school again. For example, Hebron Academy describes its extracurricular activities and their effects as follows:

The outing club organizes one or two trips each weekend which include canoeing, kayaking, overnight camping, snowshoeing, cross-country skiing, and woodscraft of all types. Through these activities students develop and perfect new skills. The exhilaration and confidence gained in mastering any one of these pursuits after experiencing frustration in other areas can, and often does, result in significant changes in attitudes and improved performance in many other areas.

For many students, extracurricular activities provide some of the strongest satisfactions of their school years, as the last quote suggests. The experiences in various activities allow students to explore their own interests, do things they like to do, and develop their skills. The activities also can often be a way for students with varied backgrounds and academic talents to meet each other on an equal basis, and can lead to lasting friendships. For these reasons, this study was concerned with the extracurricular program, the arts, and the use of free time.

Overall, as shown in Table 4-3, the majority of students seem to be reasonably satisfied with the extracurricular and athletic programs at their schools. The majority of students, teachers, and administrators felt that the extracurricular programs at their schools have sufficient variety, scope, and quality, and that students have freedom to develop their own extracurricular activities. The majority also felt that there was enough variety in the athletic program, that the athletic program meets the needs of students who are not especially gifted athletically, and that athletics were *not* too strongly emphasized at their schools. However the majority of students and many teachers and

Table 4-3
Attitudes Toward Extracurricular Activities and Related Matters
(in percentages)

| | Group | | | | | |
| | Students | | Teachers | | Administrators | |
Items	D*	A	D	A	D	A
The extracurricular program has sufficient variety, scope, and quality	38	58	20	78	17	81
Students have freedom to develop their own extracurricular activities	35	60	12	84	9	88
There is enough variety in the athletic program	19	75	16	78	18	80
There should be more opportunity for informal sports	25	58	41	44	45	46
The athletic program meets the needs of students who are not especially gifted athletically	35	57	30	61	32	62
Athletics are too strongly emphasized at this school	56	38	72	22	76	20
Students have ample free time for nonrequired activities	53	40	31	64	24	70
There is too much free time at this school	85	6	74	21	74	21
This school helps students make productive use of their free time during the school year	50	35	40	52	47	44

Source: *Questionnaire for Students, Teachers and Administrators* and *Questionnaire for New Students*, Educational Testing Service and the Secondary School Research Program, © 1971, 1972, Educational Testing Service.

*D = Strongly disagree or Disagree; A = Agree or Strongly agree; Not Shown = No opinion and no response

The item read as follows: For the items below, please indicate how strongly you agree or disagree with each statement about your school.

administrators also felt that there should be more opportunity for informal sports.

Since one of the most important parts of the extracurriculum is the area of the arts, questions about facilities and participation in those areas were included in this study. The majority of every group thought that at their school the opportunities were adequate in theater, music, painting and graphics, photography and films, and creative writing. Opportunities in sculpture and crafts were considered inadequate more often than adequate. The majority of students and many teachers and administrators had been spectators in the same five areas that were described as having adequate opportunities. More than a quarter of the students had been creators or performers in creative writing, music and theater.

The answers to some other questions about free time and privacy asked of people in independent schools were enlightening. The majority of students in these schools *did not* feel that students had ample free time for nonrequired activities, and did not feel there was too much free time at their schools. Half felt that their schools did not help students make productive use of their free time during the school year. Teachers and administrators also did not feel there was too much free time at the school, but did think students had ample free time for nonrequired activities.

The general level of satisfaction with extracurricular activities and athletics is suggested by the rather small number of critical comments about these areas. One area *did* receive a good many comments, however. This area was the use of free time. Some students commented that there was free time, but that it was poorly spaced.

My school provides free time but not in large enough blocks to accomplish much.

The free time given is given in short spans. Ten minutes here, thirty minutes there. There is rarely a long, free length of time in which the student is free from all obligations. The student, should he so desire, can participate in the school's extracurricular activities, but has little or no opportunity to do things that he desires which are not offered by the school.

Others felt that the emphasis on academic success conflicted with the use of free time.

I feel that because of excessive homework, I am pressured and as a result do not have as much free time as I would like. However, this pressure may be because of my inability to finish the work which others can finish quite easily.

We heard many comments to this effect. As we have suggested earlier, the academic pressures of the schools may not allow students much time to follow their own interests or develop their nonscholastic talents. Some schools' devotion to one form of excellence may create environments which make it hard for other forms of excellence to flourish. The extracurricular program at least provides students with opportunities to relax from the pressures for academic achievement. For some students extracurricular activities are a powerful learning experience, which helps them to develop and increase their talents, and encourages them to believe in their ability to handle difficult tasks in areas they value.

Counseling

The goals of counseling are lofty ones (Bragdon, 1965). They are based on the assumption that the purpose of education is to develop each individual to his or her fullest capacity, both for his or her own welfare and for the good of society. The variation in the abilities, interests, and aims of students requires their individual treatment so that their potential may be realized. The increased complexity of life means that it is increasingly difficult to adjust to life in the school, the home, and the external society. Well-trained counselors can help the student cope with life and make appropriate educational and vocational decisions. In these times it is especially important for students to talk to understanding and well-informed adults who can respond to them as individuals with individual needs and problems. Of course, in the elite schools, many adults other than the formal counseling staff are available for this kind of personal guidance. Teachers and housemasters see their students every day, play sports with them, share meals with them, and help them with classwork. Only a few of these people have extensive training in counseling, but most are friendly and accessible. For this reason, "counseling" was defined quite broadly in this study to include the many informal sources of help, as well as the formal ones, although we also specifically asked about the effectiveness of formal counseling. In general, we were concerned with the question "Does counseling performance live up to counseling rhetoric?"

As reports by Tyler (1961) and Volsky et al. (1965) have indicated, the evaluation of counseling is a complicated task. The questions we asked did not provide all the information needed to completely study the counseling services, but they did provide systematic information about how the people in the schools evaluate those services. Students see counselors for many reasons: advice about colleges and careers, test results, personal problems, etc. We attempted to discover how well the counseling services are doing their job by asking three questions: (1) When students feel they need advice, to whom do they turn? (2) When students turn to the formal counseling or guidance services in their school, how satisfactory do they feel it is? and (3) In what areas would students, teachers, and administrators like to see their school provide counseling or other forms of help?

1. To whom would students turn if they felt they needed advice? When students were asked this question, they were provided with a list of seven persons (teacher, school counselor, parent, another student, house or dorm master, doctor or clergyman, some other adult) and "no one; don't know." These choices were provided for fourteen areas (see Table 4-4). The most frequently chosen person was another student, chosen most frequently in four areas: personal problems, trouble in adjusting to school, relations with the opposite sex, and drugs. Parents were chosen in three areas: choosing an occupation, solving financial problems, and finding a job after graduation. Teachers were chosen in the areas of trouble with classwork and trouble with reading or study skills. "No one" or "don't know" were chosen in three areas:

Table 4-4
Person to Whom Students Would First Turn if They Felt They Needed Advice in Various Areas
(in percentages)

Area	Person							
	Teacher	School Counselor	Parent	Another Student	House or Dorm Master	Doctor or Clergyman	Some Other Adult	No One Don't Know
Trouble in adjusting to the school	11	14	20	31	9	1	2	9
Advice about college admission	8	73	8	2	1	0	2	3
Trouble with classwork	74	4	3	9	2	0	0	4
Relations with the opposite sex	1	0	13	54	1	2	3	20
Personal problems	3	1	27	36	2	2	4	19
Choosing an occupation	3	13	35	3	0	1	8	29
Trouble with reading or study skills	61	11	4	1	1	0	1	14
Finding a job during school	3	20	20	5	2	0	9	32
Solving financial problems	0	7	56	4	1	0	3	23
Finding a job after graduation	1	10	35	4	0	0	17	26
Ethical or moral problems	2	1	25	24	1	10	4	26
Drugs	2	2	16	37	1	9	5	23
Trouble with a teacher	21	23	16	17	6	1	3	8
Racial problems	3	4	15	22	2	3	4	39

Source: *Questionnaire for Students, Teachers and Administrators* and *Questionnaire for New Students*, Educational Testing Service and the Secondary School Research Program, © 1971, 1972, Educational Testing Service.

The item read as follows: (Students only) If you felt you needed advice in any of the following areas, who would be the *one* person in each area you would most likely turn to first for advice?

finding a job during school, ethical or moral problems, and racial problems. These results suggest that students turn to people they are most familiar and friendly with, persons they feel they can trust. Independent school students probably felt that working during school and racial problems were hypothetical situations that did not apply to their experience so they were unsure about whom they would turn to. Students seem to feel that they must solve their ethical or moral problems alone.

School counselors were the most frequently chosen in only two areas: advice about college admission (73 percent) and trouble with a teacher (27 percent). In six areas, they were chosen by less than 5 percent of the students: trouble with classwork, relations with the opposite sex, personal problems, ethical or moral problems, drugs, and racial problems. It appears that students see counselors as sources of information about colleges, and occasionally, as the person they would talk to if they had problems with a teacher—there may be no one else who would have power to influence the teacher. But in several areas in which counselors feel they have particular skill—dealing with personal and moral problems, helping students develop their skills for successful classwork—few students said they would turn to a counselor first. And in an area where most counselors feel considerable expertise, choosing an occupation, only 13 percent of students said they would turn to a counselor first. In sum, for most students, their school counseling services were seldom a primary source of help, except for advice about colleges.

It is striking that, with the exception that students turn to teachers when they have trouble with their studies, students do not turn to any of the other adults in the school. Teachers, house or dorm masters, doctors or clergymen would be asked for advice by very few students. The results for house or dorm masters go against the expectations of many adults in the schools. They feel that the housemaster is the confidant, friend, and guide to the students in his or her charge, and that the housemaster, in fact, acts almost as a parent to the students. One housemaster told me that he expected that at least half the students would say they would turn to him first. However, housemasters would be turned to for advice by less than 10 percent of the students for *any* problem. The same results held for doctors and clergymen, and for other adults (except for finding a job). Thus the students would not turn to the schools' staff for most problems, whether the staff were part of the schools' formal or informal counseling program.

2. When students do turn to counselors, how do they evaluate the counseling offered? The results of the items about this question reveal a considerable lack of knowledge about the counseling facilities on several items. Many students replied that they had no opinion, did not know, or could not respond to several items: 54 percent on "helping students solve their financial problems," 48 percent on "helping students find jobs," 47 percent on "helping students choose appropriate occupations," and 34 percent on "helping students with serious emotional problems." How satisfactory do students who do respond find counseling? The highest rating the counseling services received was on the item "advising students about colleges," which 29 percent described as "very satisfactory." But 29 percent of the students also described it as *unsatisfactory*. And in five of ten areas the majority of the students who had any opinion about the counseling services described them as unsatisfactory. These areas were "helping solve students' personal problems," "helping students choose appropriate occupations," "helping students solve their financial problems," "helping students find jobs," and "helping students with serious emotional problems."

Compared to students, teachers and administrators more often expressed opinions about counseling services at their schools and were generally more satisfied with them. However, the differences between the groups were generally not large, except for two items: 46 percent of the teachers and 51 percent of the administrators described their schools' counseling services as very satisfactory in advising students about colleges, as against 29 percent of the students; 48 percent of the students, as against 25 percent of the teachers and 22 percent of the administrators described their counseling service as unsatisfactory in helping solve students' personal problems. Taken together, these figures suggest that students are generally dissatisfied with school counseling services in most areas. Of course, many schools may not be prepared to provide counseling in all these areas. But even in areas where one would expect the counseling services to have considerable expertise, such as helping students choose occupations, they tended to be rated low by students. And if students feel they cannot turn to the counseling service for help in some of these areas, who *can* they turn to in the school community?

Perhaps, as one student commented, "Every school should have a resident psychiatrist. Too much emphasis is put on reward and *punishment*, not enough on guidance." In some schools the counseling services may serve a disciplinary role that is antithetical to their goal of helping students. In any case, many schools in the sample may not be able to do the kind of job they would like to do for reasons like those described by one teacher, who said there are reasons ". . . for conditions which would produce an unsatisfactory answer. In this case, it is lack of time due to inadequate number of staff, more emotional and drug problems, and a college-oriented community with little or no vocational counseling being done or desired."

3. In what areas would people in these schools like to see counseling provided? The majority of students would like to see their school provide counseling in two areas: drugs and choosing an occupation. The majority of teachers would like to see counseling in those same areas plus four other areas: relationships between the sexes, drinking, honesty with other people, and the application of ethical values to everyday life. The majority of administrators would like to see their school provide counseling in all those areas plus two others: the relation between the individual and society, and relations between the races. In brief, most administrators would like to see counseling in every area, teachers in most areas, and students in just two of eight areas. No wonder counselors sometimes feel they are asked to do everything.

In contrast to the differing views about counseling, the majority of all three groups would like to see their school offer *courses* on the relation between the individual and society, and relations between the races. Few people in any group favored courses in any of the other areas, except for courses in relationships between the sexes, favored by about 43 percent of all groups combined. Similarly, the majority of every group would like to see their school provide *information* in four areas: relationships between the sexes, drugs, drinking, and choosing an occupation. Thus, the majority of *every* group would like to see their schools provide either information, counseling or courses in every area except honesty with other people and the application of ethical values in everyday life. Few people in any group thought their school should do nothing in any area.

Comments on the need for advice helped illuminate the statistics a great deal. Students felt the issues involved were very important. For example: "These are the things perhaps schools should concentrate more on rather than discipline and even some required courses." But others felt that their schools already provided the needed service, or that the school provided help by its very nature. For example, one student commented on the idea of guidance in honesty: "Honesty with other people is not something that can be covered by 'Information, Counseling, Courses' but does make up a part of what the school should offer."

However, the greatest number of comments were about *how* such counseling, information, or courses should be provided. For example, some students were concerned with the rights of the individual. "When you mention these things in this section I hope it means the information will be available. I do not think that any of these things should be pressed on people. It should be up to the individual." Others were concerned with brass tacks: "Do you mean a regular academic course taken for credit or a ½ year pass-fail or a seminar type lecture series for no credit." "Topics should be incorporated by the teachers into present courses." "A type of sensitivity course that would break down superficial inhibitions and fears is necessary." And some wanted reality, not advice: "I go to an all boys school and we do not need information, we need dances and girls themselves."

Several students commented that these programs must be truly informative, and free from value judgments:

Every answer is no because courses like these generally *tell* the student how to act in that area. For example, the study of marriage in psychology and drugs and alcohol in health are just ways of telling students what to do.

And some felt that adults in the school were so hypocritical that advice must come from outside the school.

The mere thought of some facist pig teaching me about drugs (or race or ethics or individuality or occupation or honesty, etc.) or some horny teacher telling me about girls is enough to make me sick, yet there's nothing I'd rather have than an opportunity to talk *honestly* with older people about these and other things.

I don't feel the school should do anything in the areas of sex or drugs unless it is given by someone from outside the school. The people in this school are incapable of relating to the students in these areas.

Perhaps some of the newer forms of counseling, widely used at the college level, might alter the sad picture of counseling in the elite schools. Group counseling, encounter groups, contractual arrangements, and better training of counselors could all improve the counseling in independent schools. (Some of these techniques can be seriously misused, so this should not be considered a blanket endorsement.) More important than improving the counseling staff, however, is the sensitization of teachers and administrators to the needs, pressures, problems, and anxieties their students often face. The intensity of the elite school experience can lead students to cope with pressures in many ways. If the adults in the schools were alerted to the ways that are destructive to students, and were alert to the signs of pressure, they could offer a sympathetic ear to their students, or, at the very least, understand their students a little better. Insightful and understanding teachers have done a great deal to help students in the past; the most appealing plan to improve counseling in the future would be to increase their numbers. They would not only be providing more counseling, but the counseling would be more available and would probably be used more. Students often talk with their teachers as it is; if the teachers seemed understanding of their needs, the students might naturally start to discuss their problems. Students know their teachers; they often do not know their formal counselors. There is no stigma from talking with a teacher: however, many students feel they may be labeled as deviant if they seek formal counseling. As we enter the age of "psychological man" (Rieff, 1959), a psychologically sensitive environment may become more common, so that teachers may be more willing to provide counseling, and students may put more trust in them.

Conclusions

Students were generally quite satisfied with the teaching and the academic programs of their schools. They described their teachers as friendly, thorough, and fair. They felt that the extracurriculum was satisfactory, when they could find time to participate. Academically, the schools seem first-rate. However, there were some indications that the schools may place too *much* emphasis on the academic progress of their students, to the point that students have little time for individual interests, creative expression, or just plain youthful high spirits. It appears that relationships between students and teachers and administrators were based almost entirely on the academic. Perhaps this one-sided emphasis explains why most students would seek help from adults in the schools only for academic problems. We shall return to this point in later chapters.

5

The Formal Structure of the Schools

The independent school is a complex organization, which consists of three main groups which interact in complicated ways: the students, the teachers, and the administrators. Parents, trustees, and alumni also influence the school, but the character of daily life in the school is chiefly determined by the three groups that live there. The prescribed ways in which they interact is the formal structure of the school—procedures, questions of authority and power to make decisions, and rules and regulations. The operation of the structure of the schools involves questions of communication and legitimacy. Obviously, the formal structure of the school plays a very important role in the success or failure of its programs. A school with well-designed procedures, clear and fair channels of authority and power, widely accepted rules, and effective communication among the people in the school will more successfully educate its students and be a better place for its faculty to educate them than a school with irksome procedures, capricious authority, burdensome rules, and poor communication. The purpose of this chapter is to examine these aspects of the elite schools and their effects on life in the schools.

Power in the Schools

Who runs the schools? Who do people think run the schools? The answers to these related, but different questions are important in several ways. Social psychologists have shown that power relations have a pervasive effect on groups. In particular, researchers have found that when individuals feel they have no influence on a group or institution in which they are required to stay, they tend to have less liking for the institution, have less loyalty to it, are less likely to voluntarily meet its demands without supervision, are more likely to resent it, and often show a high rate of disruptive or defiant behavior. Those people who feel they have little influence on what happens in their school may give up hope of having any say and withdraw from active participation or they may tend to regard the whole enterprise as illegitimate, as a one-way street. Clearly, power and the perception of power (and the two are often strikingly different) are important parts of the school environment. For these reasons we elicited the views of students, teachers, and administrators about the influence various persons and groups have on how the school is run.

In this study we asked each person how much say or influence various

71

groups had on the way their schools were run. As can be seen in Table 5-1, students described three groups as having "a great deal of influence" on how their school was run: the principal or headmaster (88 percent), the trustees (76 percent), and teachers (59 percent). Teachers themselves did not so often feel they had a great deal of influence (50 percent), and the majority described only the principal or headmaster as having a great deal of influence (85 percent). In contrast, the majority of administrators thought that teachers (65 percent) and headmasters (89 percent) had a great deal of influence. It is fairly clear that the headmaster or headmistress is seen as the most powerful person in the school.

The majority of all the groups say that the public has little or no influence on how the school is run. But more important are the results that 36 percent of the students felt that *students* have little or no influence, and 36 percent felt that the student government has no or little influence. Teachers and administrators thought that students had at least some influence. Thus many students feel they have little say about decisions made in their schools, in contrast to the views of teachers and administrators.

Table 5-1
Perceptions of Sources of Power in the School
(in percentages)

| | Group | | | | | | | | |
| | Students | | | Teachers | | | Administrators | | |
Sources	L*	S	G	L	S	G	L	S	G
Teachers	6	29	59	6	42	50	6	24	65
Students	36	48	13	9	59	30	4	63	28
Student government	36	46	14	19	60	15	13	60	23
Principal or headmaster	2	7	88	1	10	85	0	6	89
School superintendents	14	9	21	10	2	8	11	3	8
Other administrators	8	23	40	8	27	41	5	35	47
School board or school trustees	5	11	76	8	40	43	13	41	37
Graduates and alumni	32	38	18	33	48	8	42	47	4
The public	66	15	5	66	16	1	75	9	1
Parents	29	47	18	30	53	10	29	59	6

Source: *Questionnaire for Students, Teachers and Administrators* and *Questionnaire for New Students*, Educational Testing Service and the Secondary School Research Program, © 1971, 1972, Educational Testing Service.

*L = Little or no influence; S = Some influence; G = A great deal of influence; Not shown = Don't know and no response

The item read as follows: (To be answered by everyone) In general, how much say or influence do you feel each of the following groups has on *how your school is run?*

The responses of students to this item are reinforced by their comments. What is most ironic is that the students have the least voice and influence of all the people involved in the school, and it is for them the school is being run.

It seems as if the headmaster is the ruler of the school and the opinions of many teachers and students are sometimes not even considered. Also many alumni and parents take interest in the school but to my knowledge their opinions are not fully considered.

The board of trustees and the headmaster of the school have all the influence concerning how this school is run. This is a SCHOOL, not a goddam corporation—and administrators—the headmaster—wonder why they incur resentment from students. If administrators want power—as our headmaster craves—let them satisfy their egos in some corporation not in a school.

Parents, graduates, alumni, and students are growing in unrest—the trend of headmaster control should and perhaps will change.

Another student felt that "trustees hold the money, the power, and the backward or at least conservative ideas that hold us back." In contrast to the comments above, students in some schools described their schools as democracies. "We have a town meeting type of government. The whole community is part of the government."

Three related items add perspective to the question of student influence. When asked if "students in this school exercise real leadership in areas affecting students," 45 percent of students disagreed, 48 percent agreed. Two-thirds of the teachers and administrators agreed. When asked if "students have a reasonable opportunity to influence change in the school," 41 percent of the students disagreed, 56 percent agreed. Some 88 percent of teachers and 93 percent of administrators agreed. When asked if "students should have a voice in determining the curriculum," 89 percent of students agreed, 57 percent strongly. Only 20 percent of teachers and 18 percent of administrators strongly agreed. The picture that emerges from these items is that students, as a group, feel they have *some* influence on their school, but feel they legitimately should have more. The difference between their views and those of teachers and administrators suggest that students may press for more influence, and administrators and teachers may wonder why.

Some Realities of Power in the Schools

There is little doubt that the headmaster is the key figure in almost all the elite schools. Most schools do not spend a great deal of money on administration, so the head is often most of the administration, although he or she may be assisted by teachers who help in certain areas. In any case the head is clearly the most important person in the *formal* power structure. In most schools the head is also most important person informally. The head ". . . provides the vital presence that holds students, teachers, and administration in a constructive working relationship. He is the bond that makes things work by giving both spirit and direction to the enterprise" (Kraushaar, 1972). Although many things contribute to a schools' morale, ". . . the spirit pervading a school will not be vigorous and sustained unless the head lends vitality and direction to all its endeavors" (Kraushaar, 1972). He or she is the source of authority, a disciplinarian, school booster, and sometime friend to students. Some heads continue to teach, many advise and counsel students, and virtually all heads have to deal with special problems in student conduct. Of course, they attend most school activities and sports events, and play a large role in school ceremonies. To teachers the head is also the paymaster, personnel department, curriculum planner, manager, and public relations department. A school head spends a good deal of time in faculty meetings, committees, and discussions with teachers, during which he is the authority. To trustees, he runs the school and is its ambassador, but he is accountable to them. Thus, the multiple duties of the head make him the center of communication and activity within the school. He is necessarily the final authority, which often means he must deal with disagreements in policy before they require him to use his final authority. Since authority used too often loses its legitimacy, and because the interrelationships among the people in the school are close, the head needs to be trusted and liked. Thus, he or she needs to be on good terms with key staff members. In short, the school head usually has the greatest organizational power and the greatest personal responsibility in the school.

Independent school teachers are concerned with the way their schools are run, particularly in the areas of the curriculum, scheduling, admissions, and student discipline. Most teachers wish to have a say in these areas, and they are particularly careful to assert their control over their freedom in the classroom. In these areas they usually do hold a good deal of power.

The trustees usually have the legal power and duty to review and approve budgets, oversee the general operations of the school, to select the school head, and, in times of crisis, to radically alter the school. However, the trustees seldom influence the everyday decisions made in the schools, except through the general policies they set.

The students tend to feel relatively powerless in comparison to the adult groups in the school. They have little say in making the budget, designing the curricula, setting requirements, and, perhaps most important, defining the goals of the school. In the late 1960s, there were student movements on many campuses to change the traditional pattern. As reviewed by Blackmer (1970), these movements were often disorganized and poorly focused, although they were intense and sincere. The lack of precision may have been because

... at bottom, this demand for "voice" derives not from simple power-seeking, but from an intense longing to be listened to with respect, to be treated as grown up and taken seriously. The deep, pressing psychological need is not to *make* decisions but to contribute to their making, to count for something as a person, to be trusted and given more responsibility for the conduct of one's life. It is part of a much larger desire to establish friendly, open relations with the faculty (Blackmer, 1970: 29).

The specific proposals cited by Blackmer do seem to deal with these needs. A number of schools have responded to the student proposals in a variety of ways, as recorded by Blackmer and various articles in *The Independent School Bulletin.* The response has included accelerating the movement toward coeducation, relaxing dress and grooming rules, making athletics voluntary, increasing independent study credits, and increasing the variety and scope of the courses available. However, schools have responded much less strongly to students' desire for more flexible daily schedules, or to their demand for a share in the decision making process. What "a share" and "decision-making process" mean is not completely clear, but according to Kraushaar's results, trustees and teachers are not eager to give students a very large role. (They also believed that the school head should have the power to revoke the selection of particular student leaders.) Kraushaar seems to argue that this is due to the teachers' and administrators' present difficulties in dealing with critical, questioning, and sometimes disrespectful students. The potential problems of giving students a formal position of power or influence may loom too large in the minds of the adults in the school to make them enthusiastic about the idea.

Of course, in theory, there are many benefits from the inclusion of students in the committees and groups that make decisions for the school. If students had helped make decisions they would be more likely to seek their implementation. For example, instead of resisting rules on discipline and behavior, students should help enforce them. Students should feel less alienated and feel that their own efforts can have an impact on institutions and events. Students' sense of competence, and consequently their initiative should increase. Students and teachers and administrators should gain an understanding of each other and should learn to work with each other more effectively and with greater mutual respect. Tension within the school should decline as a consequence.

In contrast to these theoretical advantages, the practical problems of student participation in decision-making are ample. Students, teachers, and administrators may hold distorted perceptions of each other, feel inadequate or anxious when dealing with each other, and encounter bureaucratic obstacles to their effective cooperation. All participants need to develop their general interpersonal sensitivity for working with others, and need to become knowledgeable about each others' roles, duties, needs, and characteristics. All participants need to develop skills in communicating with others in their own constituencies as well as skills in negotiating with the other groups. Each group needs to develop effective strategies for using influence in its school. Finally, teachers and especially school heads need to develop the ability to accept the influence of individuals and groups that they usually consider as subordinates. Even with these skills, the tasks are not easy. The actual problems of the schools are, of course, often hard to solve. In addition, some schools have found that Blackmer's (1970) projection is coming true (student demands for a share in decision-making): ". . . might become more moderate and restrained as students come to recognize that sharing in decision making and in carrying out decisions is hard, grinding work, involving responsibility of a high order as well as a great deal of time, more than they may be willing or able to give it" (p. 79). Thus, students may drop off the committees they worked so hard to be on.

In any case, a number of schools have tried various experiments in involving students in decision-making. Most students wish to be responsible, in some way, for their school's community. At the least they wish to help shape decisions, although some would like to help make decisions. Some of the experiments have already failed, some appear to be successful and most are continuing: the final results are not in. How they will come out will depend on many aspects of the school, including our next topic, communication.

Communication in the Schools

Because of the intensity and closeness of the independent schools, communication among its members is very important. People who must interact with each other on such intimate terms need to know what others are thinking and feeling so that their relations may be harmonious. People in the elite schools communicate to inform, influence, guide, interact with, and evaluate each other. Communication in the elite schools may also be said to be used for the purpose of group maintenance—that is, to express personal reactions to others, to encourage, listen to, empathize with, and show respect or disrespect for others in the school. In organizational studies, communication has been related to the effectiveness of the organization, morale, role-relations, and the formation of subgroups. Studies have also shown that people tend to try to communicate upward in the status and power hierarchies. When conditions are unfavorable, communication upward is accompanied by the costs of anxiety over possible rejection from those higher up and from peers. Those of higher status, such as teachers and administrators, tend to communicate with one another rather than downward, particularly if they see their roles as antagonistic to those of students. There is a tendency for people of different status and roles to have poor communications with one another, yet the lines of communication are crucial for the effectiveness of an institution. Thus, communication in independent schools 'must be upward, downward, and sideward; schools with only downward communication have no real communication at all. According to experience in many types of schools, the views of reality held by people with different roles are significantly different. Who is right does not matter much. The important point is whether or not effective communication has been established. Of course, sheer transmission of information is only a small part of communication. Communication means understanding other people and knowing others' needs, goals, perceptions, and ways of doing things. For these reasons, it is important to assess the quality of communication in the schools. We therefore asked students, teachers, and administrators to describe how good the communication or understanding between various persons and groups was at their school.

The figures in Table 5-2 show that the majority in every group described communications between most groups as good. Students described communica-

Table 5-2
Quality of Communication between Groups and Individuals
(in percentages)

| | Group | | | | | | | | |
| | Students | | | Teachers | | | Administrators | | |
Areas of Communication	P*	F	V	P	F	V	P	F	V
Student leaders with other individual students	21	46	22	13	55	17	15	55	17
Groups of students with other groups of students	34	46	15	19	58	9	18	54	15
Individual students with other individual students	8	44	42	6	47	38	7	41	39
Students of one race with students of another	20	37	28	21	44	24	17	56	14
Teachers with individual students	16	47	32	4	45	47	3	40	50
Teachers with student groups	31	46	15	15	58	21	11	58	21
Teachers with other teachers	14	27	19	20	42	34	11	59	23
Administrators with individual students	46	32	13	21	45	24	11	47	35
Administrators with student groups	50	31	8	22	48	20	18	53	22
Administrators with teachers	20	24	14	32	39	25	22	45	26
Counselors with students	28	36	19	14	41	26	9	45	32
Parents with the school	41	27	9	20	47	15	12	52	20

Source: *Questionnaire for Students, Teachers and Administrators* and *Questionnaire for New Students*, Educational Testing Service and the Secondary School Research Program, © 1971, 1972, Educational Testing Service.
*P = Very poor or Fairly poor; F = Fairly good; V = Very good; Not shown = Can't say and no response.
The item read as follows: (To be answered by everyone) *In general*, how good is the communication or understanding between the following persons or groups at your school?

tion between individual students, and between teachers and individual students as the best. Teachers felt the same way, and also felt that their own communications with student groups were quite good. Many students felt they could not assess the communications between teachers or between teachers and administrators, but about half the students described communications between administrators and individual students and between administrators and student groups as fairly poor or very poor. In short, students felt they have good communications among themselves and with teachers, but often felt they had poor communications with administrators. In contrast, administrators and teachers tended to think they have fairly good communications with everyone. How can such a large discrepancy between the views of administrators and students be explained? Perhaps because administrators must spend much of their time in their offices, in meetings, and dealing with outside groups, they have limited opportunities to communicate with many students or in much depth with any particular student. Unfortunately these job duties and lack of opportunities for interaction lead to the administrator's misperceptions and the student skepticism suggested above, or even to resentment, such as that expressed by one student, "In general, the administration has put itself above the students. They never have informal communication with the kids. The principal is a true politician—never says anything."

As asserted above, communication is important to the school. The importance of good communication for morale is suggested by the comment of a student "Communication at my school is at a standstill. No one cares enough to try to understand someone else's point of view." As another student pointed out it is also important to remember the difference "between the *extent* and the quality of understanding and communication."

There are problems in improving communication. Gaines (1972), for example, has offered his opinion that many teachers and administrators are actually ignorant and naive about most of the vital concerns of students: drugs, pollution, race relations, mass media, music, cinema, Eastern and mystical religious experiences, hobbies, the military complex, sexism, the new sexual morality, the erosion of freedom under a voracious government, the possibilities for communalism, anarchism and other social organizations, and racism and violence among police, among others.

The great majority of educators maintain a quite remarkable isolation from those cultural forces most powerfully influencing their students. Many even take pride in their isolation—sort of like those old English colonial officials who went off to live in the far corners of the world but scorned learning the languages of the "natives." I don't think it's necessary for every teacher to become a devotee of the Rolling Stones or an authority on Andy Warhol's films; but common sense suggests that if you're engaged in any sort of educational effort with adolescents, you ought to know something about the books they're reading, the music they're listening to, the films they're watching.

To have the adults in the school contend that these concerns are unimportant encourages students to believe that their teachers do not understand them. To have the adults contend that the narrow subjects and academic approach that *they* favor are the truly important things leads students to feel their teachers are out of touch with reality. As Gaines puts it, ". . . because we refuse to recognize the changed nature of experience, we still require passes to go to the john in high schools from kids who have spent summers working in kibbutzim in Israel or hitchhiked across a continent or marched in peace demonstrations or tutored children in the ghettos."

Another problem is that many adults in the elite schools limit discussions to the intellectual side of communication. Disclosure of feelings, personal views, and emotions are to be avoided. Yet many students believe that these things are the most important ones to communicate and understand. Some adults, particularly in administration, may resort to bureaucratese when talking to students (and to teachers). The "diplomatic" reluctance to speak plainly or to take a stand, and the use of the ambiguous compromise make communication between students and adults difficult at the least, and results in mutual distrust at the worst.

It is clear that communication will not improve simply because people would like it to. Communication, to be effective in the schools, needs to be about some things that are not usually discussed, in a language not usually used, and on a personal basis that many school people may find uncomfortable. However, if the successes of the schools that have made a concerted effort to improve communication are typical, the attempt would be worth it.

Rules and Regulations

Despite the fact that all social organizations require some rules of conduct so that the organization can function, independent schools have been criticized for having too many rules, and rules that do not really help. Although the ultimate goal of rules and discipline is the development of self-control and self-discipline within the school, the actual result is often irritation and resentment. Since one of the purposes of the schools is to help students become responsible adults, students often feel that they should be treated as adults, but feel that the school rules treat them as children. In contrast, teachers and administrators in independent schools usually feel that rules are needed to keep a minimum of order in their schools, especially since the schools must assume many responsibilities for the welfare of the students. Given these different viewpoints, it seems essential to obtain information about attitudes toward school rules.

The students, teachers and administrators in all of the schools in the study were asked to rate rules in twenty areas, indicating whether they thought the rule not strict enough, about right, too strict, or, if no rule existed, whether a rule should or should not exist. (Additional questions, asked in the boarding schools, are discussed later.) As shown in Table 5-3, there was *agreement* between a majority of all groups that rules were about right in only eight areas: dishonesty, discipline in the classroom, cheating, disobedience, tardiness, the use of drugs, the use of alcohol, and freedom for students to organize meetings and assemblies. It is striking that most of these rules bear on classroom behavior. Perhaps rules in the classroom are so obviously of benefit to all, that they are accepted by students, teachers, and administrators alike. But the groups did not see most rules in the same way. The majority of students thought rules were about right in only the eight areas listed above; the majority of teachers thought rules were about right in seventeen of twenty areas; and the majority of administrators thought rules were right in nineteen of twenty areas. Furthermore, the percentages supporting the rules were higher among administrators than teachers. Thus, teachers and administrators generally seem satisfied with their schools' rules. In contrast, 40 percent or more of students felt that rules are *too strict* in eight areas: hair and dress regulations, smoking (still a surprisingly heated issue at many schools), cutting classes, control of student publications, freedom to leave school during free periods, required attendance at classes, required attendance at assemblies, and required attendance at athletics or physical education. At most 12 percent of teachers and administrators feel that rules in *any* of these areas are too strict. The difference of opinion is particularly pronounced in two areas: freedom to leave school during free periods and required attendance at assemblies. These areas may be sources of contention at many schools.

In addition to these questions, the students, teachers, and administrators in independent boarding schools were asked similar questions about eleven areas that appeared to be important in boarding schools. The results were quite striking. The majority of boarding school students felt that the rules were too strict in nine of eleven areas (the exceptions were lights out and supervision of study hours). Students were particularly dissatisfied with rules on visiting with persons of the opposite sex, use of motor vehicles, required chapel attendance, and dining regulations. In contrast, the majority of boarding school teachers and administrators who responded to this question felt that the rules were about right in every one of these areas. This discrepancy in opinion may have been recognized by some schools, judging from the occasional efforts at reform. But the general conflict in attitudes toward rules may continue for many years in many others.

The comments on these items generally provide the same picture of secondary schools as those suggested by the statistical results. A few schools were described in favorable terms:

Our school has very few written rules; certain things are "understood." In general, each specific incident is treated individually, not according to a set of rules. There are many understood limitations, but few unbreakable rules.

Other schools were quite restrictive, as suggested by the simple number of rules mentioned by one student:

I feel the school should have the following rules:
1. Junior-seniors should be allowed to have radios and record players
2. No white shirts at night
3. Breakfast optional
4. Movies optional
5. Haircuts optional
6. Allowed to visit town once a week if you want
7. A second weekend for those with an 80 or above and if they keep it up another weekend is in order.
8. Sports optional unless you are a freshman or sophomore
9. Study hall in your room if you have an 80 or above.

The following comment, although referring to a particular school, may apply to many schools:

I have found our school to be much too restrictive to the point of creating apathy and strong discontent amongst the students. The administration doesn't relate to the student to a great enough extent. Our school is a world of its own uninvolved in any outside, or national affairs. It goes on trying to ignore present day problems by enforcing a set of very conservative rules thus creating a secure atmosphere for the faculty, not a relevant atmosphere for the students. The obsession with dress codes and required chapel has split the students from faculty, for as a student these issues are taboo, not to be discussed or questioned.

Some students felt that rules should be liberalized so that students would be ready for the freedom and responsibilities of adult life.

The school should constantly think of liberalizing some of its more petty rules if it expects to accomplish one of its basic functions, prepare a boy for University Life.

A few teachers seemed to feel that rules were not part of their jobs as teachers:

I have not even attempted to answer the question about rules which examines an area of school policy to which, thank goodness, I feel I need not pay detailed attention. I have my hands and mind full of academic problems, full time. In general, I feel confidence in the administrative policy regarding social and behavioral aspects of this school life. I should really prefer a stricter discipline, but recognize its impracticability in the midst of the total permissiveness of contemporary society.

Rules undoubtedly serve a number of purposes in the schools. Many of them are rational. For example, it is easier to plan regular events and organize schedules if the staff knows where the students are at most times. Rules that require students to account for their time help the school avoid liability in the event of problems. For example, the school could avoid a suit from parents

Table 5-3
Views on the Strictness of Rules
(in percentages)

| | Group | | | | | | | | | | | | | | |
| | Students | | | | | Teachers | | | | | Administrators | | | | |
	NS*	AR	TS	NN	NB	NS	AR	TS	NN	NB	NS	AR	TS	NN	NB
Hair and dress regulations	4	35	49	9	1	32	46	9	5	3	34	51	5	3	2
Smoking	5	38	49	1	1	20	61	13	1	1	16	67	11	0	1
Fighting	2	29	6	26	3	2	36	1	26	2	1	30	2	36	1
Cutting classes	5	45	42	2	1	27	58	8	1	2	24	64	3	1	2
Dishonesty	22	55	5	4	3	28	60	1	3	2	20	68	0	5	1
Discipline outside the classroom	5	42	38	7	1	33	48	5	4	2	35	51	3	3	1
Discipline in the classroom	5	68	10	9	1	5	76	1	10	2	9	72	1	8	1
Truancy	4	36	17	7	1	15	48	2	4	2	14	51	0	9	2
Tardiness	4	51	30	4	1	26	58	3	2	3	27	55	1	1	2
Cheating	15	67	5	2	2	16	69	1	2	3	16	73	0	3	1
Control of student publications	2	35	42	12	1	12	57	9	12	1	14	58	8	7	3
Use of drugs	14	52	23	1	1	19	68	4	1	1	16	74	1	0	1
Use of alcohol	7	51	30	2	1	10	74	4	1	1	8	83	1	0	0
Freedom to leave school during free periods	2	28	62	3	1	12	64	11	2	2	5	72	6	3	2
Disobedience, insubordination	6	50	25	4	1	20	66	3	2	2	20	65	0	4	2
Required attendance at classes	2	44	47	1	1	13	75	8	1	1	15	74	5	0	1
Required attendance at assemblies	3	30	60	2	1	17	65	9	1	1	18	66	7	2	1
Required attendance at athletics or physical education	4	35	52	3	1	13	63	11	5	1	12	61	11	6	1
Freedom for students to organize meetings and assemblies	1	63	17	14	1	1	76	5	10	1	2	79	3	10	0

| Freedom for students to distribute printed materials at school | 1 | 47 | 27 | 15 | 1 | 4 | 65 | 6 | 11 | 2 | 5 | 70 | 1 | 13 | 4 |

Source: *Questionnaire for Students*, *Teachers and Administrators* and *Questionnaire for New Students*, Educational Testing Service and the Secondary School Research Program © 1971, 1972, Educational Testing Service.

*NS = Not strict enough; AR = About right; TS = Too strict; NN = No rules on this, and there should not be; NB = No rules on this, but there should be.

The item read as follows: (To be answered by everyone) How do you feel about the strictness of school rules in the following areas?

whose child had been injured off campus, if the school could show that the student had violated a rule by leaving the school without permission. However, many other rules do not have such a rationale. Instead, many rules seem to have a symbolic value to adults in the school. The best examples are the hair and dress codes that have created tension and furor on many campuses. Somehow, many adults feel there is a connection between students' morality and their clothes and hair length. Perhaps at one time it was true that a leather-jacketed, long-haired student was likely to be a rebellious potential juvenile delinquent, and there was a time when short skirts were not worn by virtuous girls, but those times are long past. The link between clothes and academic or intellectual interests has nearly reversed. In the 1950s, the student with short hair, button-down collar, slacks, and well-shined shoes was likely to be the one oriented toward studies, books, and the laboratory. Today, the opposite may be true; the clean cut student is often the one who is not interested in ideas and their consequences, whereas the long-haired, blue-jeaned student often is. Neatness of clothing and hair obviously do not guarantee either morality or scholarliness. As Gaines (1972) puts it:

... I've seen too many neat, clean, scrubbed and trimmed and Brooks Brothers-attired Lawrenceville boys who were vicious bullies in the seclusion of the halls; I've seen too many paragons of courtesy—in public—who were privately selfish, cynical little snobs. It has always seemed to me that the school paid far too much attention to *manners* while virtually ignoring fundamental *morals.*

Besides the adults' traditional belief in the connection between dress and behavior, there may be another subconscious reason for dress and grooming codes in schools. The uniformity of dress and appearance provides visible evidence of the schools' control over the students. By making this control visible, the students are reminded of their position, and, theoretically, will be less rebellious. This reasoning may account for the feeling, among some adults in the school, that dress is an indication of "respect" and that long hair or sloppy clothes show "disrespect." As one woman teacher—and no conservative—said, after moving from a school with no dress code to one that had a fairly strict one, "It's kind of nice to have everyone neat and clean, and have them say 'yes, ma'am' and 'no, ma'am' when I ask them questions."

Many rules are being reviewed at many schools, and have already been changed at many schools. There seems to be a trend to loosen rules, not only because of the complaints of students but also because the schools are recognizing the relatively greater maturity of their students in the 1970s. Not all rules can or will be removed, but most schools will probably welcome a move to make their campuses more informal and relaxed places to live and study.

Summary

We have examined several aspects of the formal structure of the schools. These are important aspects, but they do not cover all the intricacies of the formal structure, which would include role relationships, finances, and details of organizational structures. However, the aspects we have studied—power, communication, and rules and procedures—seem to be the ones which are most important to the well being of the people in the schools. In each area we have found that the students seem to stand alone. They feel they have little power, have a poor level of communication with the administrators who do hold power, and believe they are the victims of restrictive and arbitrary rules. All of this indicates that students feel that they are the last people considered and consulted when a decision is made. They may feel that they are considered to be transients in a hotel, where the people who count are the management and staff. I do not believe that this feeling is just the pique of students who feel put upon. Rather, I think it is a consequence of the organizations and purposes of the schools.

6
The Philosophy of
the Schools

Some of the most important facts about the elite schools are the values they espouse and the goals they seek. These are expressions of the basic and pervasive educational philosophies of the schools. In many ways, the philosophy of the schools is the most important information about them. If one understands the philosophical underpinnings of the schools—their actual philosophies, not their claimed philosophies—one can understand many things about the schools. One can understand why decisions were made in certain ways, why the curriculum offers the courses it does, and the criteria by which individuals—students, teachers, and administrators alike—are evaluated.

In this study, we studied the philosophy of the schools in two ways. The first was to determine the values held by the individuals in the schools; we assumed that the values of the important groups in the school would help us understand the goals individuals seek in the school experience. In addition, values are an important part of the schools' images of themselves. They all believe that they stand for certain values; it may be useful to see what they are. The second approach to the philosophies of the school was to ask students, teachers, and administrators to describe the purposes or goals they felt their schools were pursuing in practice. Then, in order to assess the degree of support for these goals, we asked the individuals in the schools to describe the goals they thought their schools *should* be pursuing. Taken together, knowledge of the values and goals of the schools provides essential information about their approaches to education and their reasons for being.

Values

People in the elite schools talk a lot about "values." They may be vague about what they mean, but many of them are sure that "values" are "declining," or are in a "state of crisis," or that the schools are in danger of "losing their values." A good many policies and decisions are defended on the basis of their importance for "values." Rules against smoking cigarettes, for example, or against short skirts for girls are somehow supposed to be related to "values," though the relationship seems to be mostly rationalization. Most school heads feel that their schools should promote *the* enduring values. But these values turn out to be amazingly vague when one presses for a definition. They seem to refer to whatever it is the speaker is justifying or promoting at the moment. Furthermore, as Peter Prescott has pointed out in his fine book on Choate, there is often a confusion between true values such as courage or honesty, and manners, such as wearing a tie to dinner. He feels that the schools sometimes confuse the morals of the country club and the ethics of the Sermon on the Mount. The things most often brought up in conversations about values with teachers and administrators include courage, independence (the "responsible" kind, not the "destructive" kind), commitment, honor, courtesy, service to family, country, and world, and, in some schools, reverence and spiritual faith. There is something behind these platitudinous virtues that does have true worth, of course. But it is extremely difficult to "teach" such things, even if one does have a clear idea of the goal. It is particularly difficult to design a school environment to promote such values. As an intensive study of the influence of Jesuit schools found, even specific goals of inculcating particular beliefs are difficult to implement and even more difficult to attain (Fichter, 1969). However, because of the claimed and actual importance of values to the life of the elite schools, we tried to assess the values of the people in the schools. We also attempted to find out how much thought students had given to their values, and sought to identify the sources of students' values.

How May We Assess Values?

In every society, men strive for what they believe to be right and good. Their beliefs about what is right and wrong, important or unimportant, are their values. The system of values held by individuals or groups have, of course, an important influence on their actions. One cannot hope to understand an individual or a group without understanding his or its values. (It is beyond the scope of this report to discuss the various conceptual and research difficulties in the idea of "value," but the reader is referred to the bibliography by Albert and Kluckholm (1960) and the discussions by Smith (1963), Henry (1963), and Barry and Wolf (1967).

Values have their sources in parental training, social class, education, and personal thought and experience. Arising as they do from such fundamental sources, values assume an important role in each person's conception of himself or herself. They form internal standards by which one evaluates oneself. Measured against these standards, one's self-esteem falls or rises from shame to pride. In addition, research has shown values to be related to grades, intelligence, choice of major field, vocational interests, and occupational choice. Other research suggests that different experiences, education, or school and college environments have different influences on values. Thus, values have pervasive effects on the actions, thoughts, and emotions of persons throughout their lives. They strive for some things because for them they have value and are worth the effort. The relative importance of values at any time is a function of the person, his life situation and past experiences.

To understand a person's actions and motivations, it is essential to know the *relative* importance of his values at a given point in his life.

We approached the study of values by two techniques. In the first, the students, teachers and administrators were asked to indicate the *three* values that were most important to them from a list of thirteen values. This "forced choice" technique was used to determine what people would choose when they could only choose certain things, and could not choose everything. In the second technique, respondents could rate the personal importance of each of fourteen things they could do in their lives.

When presented with the list of values and asked to indicate the three most important, students, teachers and administrators all tended to choose two values, "being independent and original" and "being friendly to people even if they do things against your own beliefs," as shown in Table 6-1. Teachers and administrators also tended to choose the value "living your religion in your daily life." Some 46 percent of administrators and 41 percent of teachers chose this value as against only 16 percent of students. In contrast, 52 percent of students chose the value "standing up for your own rights," as against 22 percent of teachers, and 15 percent of the administrators.

Interestingly, very few (less than 14 percent) in any group chose the value "working hard to obtain academic honors." Of course, with the forced choice technique, respondents were limited in the possibilities open to them and could only say *whether* the item was important, but not how strongly they felt about it. Many respondents objected to this limited technique, since it did not include values they felt were important, and they had difficulty choosing three values. As one student said, "How the hell can one rank whether being original is more important than telling the truth?"

The difference in the item on living one's religion may be based on different conceptions of religion. Student comments suggested that if this meant traditional formal religion, they would not choose it, but if it meant a general approach to life, they would choose it. As one student commented, "Many students have a religious feeling towards 'Man cooperating with his fellow man,' but do not follow traditional lines." Another student said religion "means to me becoming a full person or living in a person centered way." It may be symptomatic that while only 11 percent of the students chose "being non-conformist, different from other people," almost none of the teachers or administrators chose this value.

The second technique was designed to present students, teachers, and administrators with the question, "What do I really want out of life?" Individuals ask themselves this question throughout their lives, and their answers change through their lifetimes, of course. The answers also vary with opportunities, vocational choices, social class, and cultural traditions. But the important point is that people want to live for something beyond themselves and prefer to be actively striving for some goals.

Research has shown that life goals are related to the central motivations in

Table 6-1

Values Chosen by Students, Teachers, and Administrators

(in percentages)

Value	Group		
	Students	*Teachers*	*Administrators*
Being friendly to people even if they do things against your own beliefs	37	41	46
Standing up for your own rights	52	22	15
Being poised, gracious, and charming no matter where you are	8	14	11
Working hard to achieve academic honors	13	13	13
Developing physical strength and skill	9	3	1
Always telling the truth even though it may hurt others' (or your own) feelings	13	23	21
Being careful with other people's property or money	18	18	27
Going out of your way to repay people for being kind to you	17	19	13
Living your religion in your daily life	15	41	46
Demanding and getting the respect you deserve	9	7	4
Replying to anger with gentleness even when you have a reason to be angry yourself	17	25	30
Being independent and original	64	54	44
Being nonconformist, different from other people	11	1	0

Source: *Questionnaire for Students, Teachers and Administrators* and *Questionnaire for New Students*, Educational Testing Service and the Secondary School Research Program, © 1971, 1972, Educational Testing Service.

The item read as follows: (To be answered by everyone) Which three of the following describe the values most important to you? Mark only the three *most* important.

our personalities. We integrate ourselves with certain goals in mind, organize our activities, take actions, and make choices on the basis of goals. The goals may be stated or unstated, but they help guide our behavior. And our evaluation of those behaviors and ourselves as successful or failing are based on goals. The compatability between a person's goals and his abilities is also important. (The interested reader will find a valuable guide to thinking and research about goals in a book by Buhler and Massarik, *The Course of Human Life: A Study of Goals in the Humanistic Perspective* (1968).)

There can be as many goals as there are people, so, to have any meaningful information about goals, we needed to focus on major goals that have long-range implications for the person. Since we also needed to work within the requirements of the questionnaire format, we needed to limit the possibilities to a workable number. The final choice of goals was based on goals that had been shown to distinguish people with different vocational choices, creative performance, academic performance, and which had been subject to earlier statistical analyses. The final fourteen goals are shown in Table 6-2.

When students, teachers, and administrators rated the separate importance of each of the fourteen life-goals, they all tended to give high importance to the same goals, and low importance to the same goals. The highest importance in every group was assigned to three goals: "have a happy family life," "find personal happiness," and "understand other people." Interestingly, the goal that

Table 6-2
The Importance of Fourteen Life Goals
(in percentages)

	Group											
	Students				Teachers				Administrators			
Goal	N*	I	V	E	N	I	V	E	N	I	V	E
Achieve financial success	33	40	15	9	33	52	7	4	30	56	3	3
Find personal happiness	1	7	24	65	2	17	34	44	2	18	36	38
Develop a philosophy of life	16	28	22	30	6	23	30	35	5	26	32	31
Make a contribution to knowledge	36	30	19	11	22	36	27	11	34	30	23	8
Engage in the performance or creation of works of art	44	25	16	13	45	29	12	8	55	25	9	4
Have the means and time to enjoy the pleasures of life	5	28	27	36	4	47	29	15	7	49	26	13
Be of service to others	5	27	32	33	2	27	39	30	1	20	39	34
Live and work in the world of ideas	17	31	25	22	7	33	29	28	11	27	33	24
Be independent of others	18	27	25	26	19	36	23	17	23	34	22	14
Become a leader in politics	81	10	4	3	88	6	1	1	81	11	2	0
Have a happy family life	5	13	26	53	4	15	30	46	2	12	28	52
Understand other people	2	12	29	54	2	17	39	38	1	12	36	45
Live my life in my own way without interference from others	24	27	19	26	30	38	18	10	32	37	16	7
Change the world for the better	13	29	27	27	11	45	25	15	14	41	26	14

Source: *Questionnaire for Students, Teachers and Administrators* and *Questionnaire for New Students*, Educational Testing Service and the Secondary School Research Program, © 1971, 1972, Educational Testing Service.

*N = Not important; I = Important; V = Very important; E = Essential

The item read as follows: (To be answered by everyone) How important is it to you to do the following things in your life?

had by far the lowest ratings of importance (over 80 percent in every group rating it "not important") was "become a leader in politics." Even in these times, when there is much talk of involvement, participatory democracy, and politicizing educational institutions, and even with the schools' rhetoric about providing "leaders to the nation," very few people in the elite schools seem to want to become leaders in politics. The second lowest rating of importance was assigned to "engage in the performance or creation of works of art." All the groups placed relatively little importance on achieving financial success, but 63 percent of the students (44 percent of the teachers, and 39 percent of the administrators) considered having "... the means and time to enjoy the pleasures of life" as important or *essential*. Epicureanism is still the prerogative of youth. It is also striking that most of the remaining goals are rated as essential by less than a third of any group, especially when their content is examined: make a contribution to knowledge, live and work in the world of ideas, be independent of others, etc. It may be encouraging to note that 54 percent of students rated the goal "change the world for the better" as very important or essential.

A number of respondents felt that some of the goals had different meanings to different people, especially "the pleasures of life," "philosohpy of life," and "change the world for the better." One student wondered whether "the pleasures of life," meant "making money and enjoying the materialistic things you can buy with money, or being able to make money so as not to have to slave away at a job 24 hours a day so that you have time to stop and enjoy Nature's beauty, contemplation, thought, the arts, etc." Another student reacted to the goal of developing a philosophy of life for reasons that may be behind the responses of many students: "It is wrong, I think, to worry about a philosophy of life. I hope to have ideas about life, but I hope more than anything else to live life and not worry about profound statements about life." Another student suggested that "change the world for the better" can become a mindless cliche. "Change the world ... is geared to prick guilty consciences; at boarding school our responsibility as the 'top 5%' of this nation (financially and intellectually) to 'change the world' is pounded into us until I would check 'not important' from sheer perverseness—constant repetition of the *words* 'change the world' induces a cynical apathy and hopeless attitude for some." Finally a student made a distinction that may help to explain why the goal of "become a leader in politics" received such a low rating: "It is not important that I become a political leader but it is essential that I be active in politics. Right now it is of primary importance to my life."

Given the general values and goals just described, how well thought out or well defined are students' standards of behavior in day-to-day affairs? To answer this question we devised the item shown in Table 6-3. The areas seemed to cover the most crucial areas of moral concern that face students today.

Students tended to say their standards of behavior were better defined than

Table 6-3
Clarity of Students' Standards of Behavior

(in percentages)

Area of Behavior	Group								
	Students			Teachers			Administrators		
	P*	F	V	P	F	V	P	F	V
Relations between the sexes	15	46	33	37	40	4	36	46	5
Drugs	10	32	54	39	39	11	42	35	13
Drinking	9	31	55	30	40	15	26	47	15
Cheating	8	20	66	20	38	35	20	32	37
Honesty with other people	5	29	61	18	46	30	23	47	25
The application of ethical values to every day life	15	42	33	38	42	10	40	44	9
The relation between the individual and society	23	42	25	40	41	9	49	38	6

Source: *Questionnaire for Students, Teachers and Administrators* and *Questionnaire for New Students*, Educational Testing Service and the Secondary School Research Program, © 1971, 1972, Educational Testing Service.

*P = Very Poorly or Poorly Defined; F = Fairly well defined; V = Very well defined; Can't say and No Response percentages are not shown.

The item read as follows:

Students—How clearly defined or well thought out do you feel your personal standards of behavior are in the following areas?

Teachers and administrators—How clearly defined or well thought out do you feel students' standards of behavior are in the following areas?

teachers and administrators did. For example, in the areas of drugs, drinking, cheating, and honesty with other people the *majority of students* said their standards of behavior were *very* well defined, while relatively few teachers and administrators thought students' standards in those areas were well defined. In the area of relationship with the opposite sex, 79 percent of the students as opposed to about half the teachers and administrators thought their standards were fairly or very well defined. In most areas few students thought that their standards were poorly or very poorly defined. For these same areas, however, much greater proportions of teachers and administrators thought students' standards were poorly or very poorly defined.

In brief, teachers and administrators tend to have a lower opinion of the clarity of students' standards than students themselves hold. It should be emphasized that this is a *relative* judgment. Most teachers and administrators who responded felt that students' standards were fairly or very well defined in every area. The students just had higher opinions of their standards of behavior.

The reasons for this discrepancy may possibly lie in the differences in standards held by students and adults. As one student commented, "Many adults will answer 'poorly defined' if the values students hold differ markedly from their own, regardless of how well defined they may be." Another student felt he had difficulty responding to the items because "I cannot accept traditional moral judgments, and as a result am having a hard time defining them." And another student pointed out that a "standard of behavior could be good without being clearly defined. For example, a student may not cheat at all, but would have a hard time defining the basis for his action." Finally, one person noted that "One can conclude, after considerable thought on these questions, to remain completely flexible regarding one's personal actions."

What are the *sources* of students' values? Who influences students? Some teachers and administrators assume their schools have a strong impact on students' values and beliefs, and they take their responsibilities quite seriously. They feel that the personal examples they present, the values they demonstrate in classes, and the time they require students to spend in chapel shape students' views of right and wrong. For example, one school contended it ". . . has held on to the premise, in a secular age, that a religious perspective on life is an advantage to personal growth and intellectual maturity. Consequently, it provides for each boy, through its curriculum and chapel, a stimulating intellectual and personal challenge by means of the broad teachings of the Christian faith." (*Independent Secondary Schools: A Handbook*, 1971)

In order to examine the influence of the school and other forces on the values of students, we designed a question which asked students to indicate the *most* important sources of their personal, ethical, and spiritual values from a list of eleven possible sources. Teachers and administrators were asked to indicate which sources they thought were most important for most students. Very few in any group (less than 17 percent) felt that community service, school courses in religion or ethics, other school courses, school counselors, films or plays were important sources of values. In contrast, the majority of every group thought that student friends and parents were important sources of values. The groups did not agree about two sources. Over half the administrators and over 40 percent of the teachers felt that teachers had an important influence on students' values, but only 21 percent of students felt this way. Some 45 percent of students but only 27 percent of teachers and 23 percent of administrators thought *reading* had an important role to play in students' values. Nearly a quarter of the students indicated "other" as a source, in contrast to less than 6 percent of teachers and administrators. This difference is probably due to the lack of any response such as "personal reflection." Finally, less than an eighth of any group indicated that a "clergyman, priest, or rabbi" was an important source of values for themselves or for most students. In sum, all respondents recognized the influence of parents and peers on students' values, and agreed that such sources as school courses and films had little influence. Students felt their own reading and thinking had more influence than adults thought, and the adults thought teachers had more influence than the students indicated. These results suggest that many students feel the school has little effect on their values, except by selecting the kinds of students who are the student's peers. (This coincides with the results in Chapter 7, where 46 percent of students say their school has neither hindered nor helped their progress in "learning to make better ethical or moral distinctions." It also coincides with results reported in Chapter 4, where fewer than 3 percent of students said they would turn to a teacher, a school counselor, or dorm master or housemaster for advice about ethical or moral problems.) Of course, teachers and administrators felt they had an impact on students' ethical values.

Students, in contrast, seem to emphasize their own thinking and reading as sources of values. As one student put it, "The most important source for moral and ethical values is *myself*, not subject to teacher and peer group influence, only subject to introspection." And another student pointed out that certain persons can influence values negatively or positively and that one must determine "whether it was agreement with or rebellion from these people that helped form values."

What are the implications of these results for the generation gap, the crisis of values, and particularly, for the life of the elite schools? First, at least for the people *in* the schools, the values of adults and students are generally the same. Like most people, they seem to make most of their decisions in order to ensure a happy personal life and good relations with other people. Such ends as academic honors, artistic work, and contributions to knowledge were chosen by few. The only sizable differences were on the importance of one's own rights and the place of traditional religion. The difference on the importance of religion may be due to the age of the students and the time the students live in. As the recent book *A Study of Generations* (Strommen et al., 1972) showed, even among church-going Lutherans, religious belief begins to drop at fifteen and reaches a low point about the age of twenty-one. Other studies have also found that religious doubt reaches its peak in the late teens, particularly among bright intellectual students.

These are secular times. Spiritual values are given a small place in most decisions. The advertising that floods our lives is based on a pervasive hedonism that would give pause to Epicurus. The violence and eroticism of the entire world is brought into our living rooms by television. Even the churches themselves have become increasingly concerned with secular issues. Many clergymen not only favor liberal political and civil rights causes, but sometimes favor such controversial ideas as premarital sex, group marriage, and legalization of marijuana. Ironically, the very concern of the churches with current affairs may turn off many students. Instead of spiritual inspiration they may find church services to be a rerun of the evening news. In contrast, the emphasis on religion in some schools with its continuous sermonizing, may also turn off students. Enforced religion may remove the enjoyment and sense of personal meaning so critical for a vital religion.

One plausible explanation of the rise of interest in fundamental, revival-style religion is that young people are tired of the gray, predictable, and unimpassioned liberalism of their churches. The unenthusiastic and partial belief of the liberal church contrasts sharply with the excitement and certainty of the fundamental evangelical movements. Rather than focusing on liberal social programs, the fundamental movements exhort their members to act now to save their own and others' souls. Instead of a morality which seems a matter of sophisticated definition, the fundamentalists present a moral code that is clear and absolute. It should come as no surprise that this certainty and enthusiasm would entrance students who had found little to move them in the religions of their childhood.

A similar explanation may apply to the importance of personal rights to students. In an environment that monitors most of their activities, that surrounds them with rules, and makes most of their decisions for them, students' reactions might naturally be to insist on their rights. In order to feel that they are active, autonomous persons on their own terms, they may feel, even if subconsciously, that they must protect their own spheres of activity. This result seems to be an indication of one of the psychological costs of the intensity of the elite schools' environment. The force of the environment creates an opposite if not equal force in the minds and behaviors of the students. This one result is a thin straw on which to base such sweeping ideas, of course. However, we presented more evidence for these ideas in the chapter on student life, and will present more evidence in the next section.

The Purposes and Goals of the Schools

Perhaps the most basic information we need to know about any school is the nature of its purposes or goals. Algo Henderson, the former president of Antioch, has written (1969) that the identification of a goal for an institution provides a valuable frame of reference for understanding the school. For example, nearly all elite school teachers will contend that their particular courses will assist in advancing students' competence in intellectual matters. We must then assume that there are pervasive goals, such as improving students' intellectual competence, that underlie each of the specific goals of the courses and of other activities in the elite schools. In practice, however, such goals are very often merely assumed. Henderson's central point is that by knowing the purposes of a school we will know better what it is striving for, what it is trying to do, be able to examine means to the achievement of goals, and be able to establish criteria that will aid this entire process. Such a critical examination of the independent schools' purposes could help us in several ways: since purposes provide a framework to examine all school activities, a serious consideration of them can help us identify the changes independent schools hope to effect in students. Identifying purposes can help us focus on what is relevant to the process of education and ignore what is irrelevant. As Peterson (1970) has pointed out, goals can be used to help formulate the institutions' policies and philosophy. When goals are stated, they can tie together people's assumptions and hopes for their institutions into coherent policies. The policies can provide guidance for decisions and actions. When we have the schools' purposes clearly in mind, we can consider the changes they are really looking for in students. This could suggest new opportunities for action, and more direct ways to accomplish the things they desire. We can then study the relation of the day-to-day work of the schools to their goals.

As Alvin Eurich (1969) has pointed out, to classify goals and establish priorities among them is the most important step in planning. If we can determine the priorities the schools assign to their various goals we can better understand how decisions are made and how resources are allocated.

By referring to their purposes, we can evaluate the schools' present programs, estimate the worth of proposed curricular and other suggested changes, and in general see how well they are doing their intended job. A clear understanding of the purposes of a school and its current activities can lead to an estimate of how well it is producing the results its purposes require.

The items used to examine school goals in this study focused on *output goals*, or goals that are "manifested in a product of some kind" (Peterson, 1970). Basically, they are concerned with the effects the school has on students' characteristics. The emphasis is on *real* rather than *stated* goals. The basic strategy is the same as that used by Gross and Grambsch (1968). Each respondent was asked to rate the extent to which each of eighteen purposes is actually emphasized at his school. Then he is asked to rate the extent to which he thinks each purpose *should be* emphasized at his school. We thought that the comparison of the "In Practice" and "Should Be" questions might suggest how well the schools were doing their job and areas where changes may be needed.

The results in Table 6-4 indicated that students, teachers, and administrators did agree that the most strongly emphasized goals in *practice* were "To help students get into college," "To prepare students for the work they will face in college," and "To help students discover and develop their intellectual abilities." They also agreed that several goals were definitely *not* emphasized: "To occupy students until they are ready for work or marriage," "To help students prepare for jobs," and "To help students improve their social and economic status." Thus, the schools are described as institutions dedicated to academic preparation, just as their catalogues say.

Students, teachers, and administrators did *not* agree on all descriptions of the purposes actually emphasized at their schools. The largest difference occurs on the item "To mold students according to society's expectations." Students thought this purpose is strongly emphasized much more often than teachers or administrators. Students also perceived more emphasis on getting students into prestigious

Table 6-4

The Perceived Purposes of the School as They Are Emphasized "In Practice"

(in percentages)

Purpose	Group								
	Students			Teachers			Administrators		
	N*	M	S	N	M	S	N	M	S
To help students improve their social and economic status	47	35	13	51	35	9	58	34	5
To help students prepare for jobs	55	29	11	64	28	3	70	26	1
To help students discover and fulfill themselves as persons	25	42	29	7	40	51	2	48	47
To help students discover and develop their intellectual abilities	7	29	62	4	20	74	1	15	84
To help students be concerned for the needs of others	31	48	17	16	59	22	12	63	23
To give students specific knowledge and skills	22	41	33	10	37	49	11	44	44
To mold students according to society's expectations	20	33	42	27	48	18	32	51	13
To occupy students until they are ready for work or marriage	73	12	8	86	7	3	92	5	0
To encourage students to be concerned more about others than about themselves	44	41	8	28	56	11	21	64	12
To help develop students' characters	19	48	27	7	50	40	8	56	33
To help students gain an understanding and respect for the rules of society	14	42	38	8	57	31	14	57	26
To prepare students to be good citizens	19	47	28	7	61	29	12	57	29
To help students get into college	3	11	84	1	14	83	4	22	73
To help students get into prestigious colleges	11	27	58	14	42	41	30	39	30
To prepare students to cope effectively with the outside world	45	35	15	20	57	20	16	63	20
To prepare students for the work they will face in college	6	23	68	4	27	67	3	30	66
To help students become intellectually independent	22	41	32	12	48	37	10	46	43
To help students develop leadership ability	24	51	19	16	56	25	16	63	19

Source: *Questionnaire for Students, Teachers and Administrators* and *Questionnaire for New Students*, Educational Testing Service and the Secondary School Research Program, © 1971, 1972, Educational Testing Service.

*N = Not emphasized; M = Moderately emphasized; S = Strongly emphasized

The item read as follows: (To be answered by everyone) First, please indicate whether you think each of the purposes below really is practiced at your school in reality.

colleges. Students were also much *less* likely to think that the schools were helping "students discover and fulfill themselves as persons" or were encouraging "students to be concerned more about others than themselves" or were preparing "students to cope effectively with the outside world." In general, these differences suggest that students, when compared to faculty and administrators, see their schools as more concerned with conformity than the development of individuals. Faculty and administrators also more often than students see their schools as emphasizing specific knowledge and skills.

What purposes do the members of the school community feel *should be* emphasized? As shown in Table 6-5, the most strongly endorsed purposes were these: "To help students discover and fulfill themselves as persons," "To help students discover and develop their intellectual abilities," "To prepare students to cope effectively with the outside world," "To help students become intellectually independent," and "To help students be concerned for the needs of others." Although 68 percent of the people in the schools believe that each of these goals should be strongly emphasized, only one, "To help students discover and develop their intellectual abilities," was described as being strongly emphasized in practice by a majority. The others were not described as strongly emphasized in practice.

Several purposes were rejected by most members of the school community: "To occupy students until they are ready for work or marriage," "To mold students according to society's expectations," "To help students improve their social and economic status," and "To help students get into prestigious colleges." We have already noted that students feel that their schools actually emphasize "molding students," and that they emphasize helping students get into prestigious colleges (as did many teachers).

There were disagreements between students and adults on purposes they would like to see emphasized. Compared to teachers and administrators, students more often thought that emphasis should be placed on "helping students prepare for jobs," and less often thought that emphasis should be placed on "helping students gain an understanding and respect for the laws of society" and "preparing students to be good citizens." Thus most members of the school community, particularly students, would like to see their schools place more emphasis on individual student growth, both personal and intellectual, and less emphasis on conformity and such traditional purposes as getting into prestigious colleges.

In general, the student, teacher, and administrator comments presented the same picture of agreement and disagreement about the purposes of the schools, what they are and what they should be. For example, one student commented on the emphasis on getting into college:

I feel that too much pressure is put on the students to get into a top school and always have straight A's. If you're not college material then you're not and you

Table 6-5
The Perceived Purposes of the School as They "Should Be" Emphasized
(in percentages)

	Group								
	Students			Teachers			Administrators		
Purpose	N*	M	S	N	M	S	N	M	S
To help students improve their social and economic status	47	34	11	60	31	3	61	30	2
To help students prepare for jobs	26	48	19	47	43	4	55	36	1
To help students discover and fulfill themselves as persons	3	9	81	0	11	84	0	8	87
To help students discover and develop their intellectual abilities	2	12	79	2	3	90	0	4	91
To help students be concerned for the needs of others	3	20	70	1	13	81	0	8	86
To give students specific knowledge and skills	11	47	34	7	45	42	8	49	38
To mold students according to society's expectations	66	21	7	42	45	6	45	42	6
To occupy students until they are ready for work or marriage	83	7	3	89	4	1	92	2	1
To encourage students to be concerned more about others than about themselves	15	36	43	8	35	51	8	26	60
To help develop students' characters	6	23	63	2	17	74	3	18	74
To help students gain an understanding and respect for the rules of society	19	51	23	3	45	47	5	36	54
To prepare students to be good citizens	19	44	28	4	34	57	4	29	63
To help students get into college	11	42	39	9	49	35	6	54	32
To help students get into prestigious colleges	49	32	11	57	32	6	58	27	6
To prepare students to cope effectively with the outside world	4	15	75	3	18	73	2	22	68
To prepare students for the work they will face in college	4	32	56	3	36	56	4	35	55
To help students become intellectually independent	4	15	74	1	11	83	2	11	80
To help students develop leadership ability	11	46	36	6	42	46	4	42	49

Source: *Questionnaire for Students, Teachers and Administrators* and *Questionnaire for New Students*, Educational Testing Service and the Secondary School Research Program, © 1971, 1972, Educational Testing Service.

*N = Should not be emphasized; M = Should be moderately emphasized; S = Should be strongly emphasized

The item read as follows: Then indicate whether you think it [the purpose] should be emphasized at your school.

can't force the idea of going to college into a person so that they will do better in grades. They are probably doing the best they can, therefore, I think we should have courses that prepare students for jobs after they graduate.

Another student pointed out that there should be more than academic preparation for college:

Most private schools really don't prepare a student for an actual profession or occupation. They mostly attempt to prepare students academically for college. If the emphasis must be on college, more emphasis should be placed upon preparation for college life, its freedoms, responsibilities, etc.

Many students seemed to feel the same way as this student, who expresses a major theme of many of the comments: "This school has prepared me academically, but morally, ethically, and religiously—nothing. It has prepared me for college, not living." This same idea was expressed vividly by one girl writing about her school: "If it is to be a good school it must also prepare students for life, not just academically, but as a housewife, mother or whatever—not a scientist, philosopher, or a female Ernie Banks."

This theme is often tied to another, that the schools are too isolated from the real world:

As a prep school student and a member of the white, male, upper middle class, I feel that the whole philosophy of the prep schools must change. It is my belief that few of the teachers and administrators truly realize the meaning of an education. Academic, book-learning education may be very good for many, but education is also experience, application of what is learned in books, and interaction with people of *both* sexes and different races. It appears that if the administrators do not realize this, the whole prep school system would die out.

Another student agreed: "I believe that the schools should become more aware of the world around them. Students are given very little opportunity to discuss and try to solve many of the problems we (the students) will have to face when we leave."

There seems to be general agreement that the schools are oriented toward academic excellence and preparation for college work. However, there are numerous large differences between the goals people feel that the schools *do* emphasize and the goals they feel they *should* emphasize. Some of the largest discrepancies—discrepancies that all school groups feel—are those on items which reflect the development of the students' capacity for caring for other people: helping students be concerned for the needs of others, and helping students to be more concerned about others than themselves. Students, teachers, and administrators alike felt that their schools should place much more emphasis than they do on helping students learn to be sympathetic and empathetic to others. These discrepancies may partly be due to the heavy emphasis on academic achievement that characterizes the schools; students and others may simply wish students could feel less pressure to see other students as competitors and more chances to see them as friends. It may also reflect the growing concern, in our society, for greater intimacy, social responsibility, and concern for the general welfare of one's community.

An area with nearly as great a discrepancy between the "is" and the "ought" was the preparation of students for coping with the outside world. By this, students seemed to mean that "real life" they felt excluded from; the result also reflected their feelings that their schools are isolated from the activities of everyday life, and that their academic preparation is often irrelevant to the real problems of the world. As one student who saw the results for her school said: "Students, teachers, and administrators saw about the same degree of discrepancy in this area, which suggests that they are all interested in making their schools' educations more applicable to the real world. The problem, of course, is to define the meaning of 'coping with the outside world.'" To some degree the feel of the real world is provided by the work study and volunteer programs on many campuses. Many schools have found that the students who tutor ghetto children, serve as assistants to local, state or national officeholders, and serve as aids in elementary schools are much more positive about their total school experience. These students generally feel they are in contact with real life. However, many of the people in the schools would like to see the schools' curriculum itself become more in line with the concerns of the modern world and include studies of ecology, population, race relations, crime, the crisis in values, and the need for intimacy in an impersonal society. Perhaps the schools could develop curricula which dealt with these issues if they lessened their concentration on getting students into college. In fact, all groups felt that their schools should place less emphasis on getting into college than they currently do. Of course, this would require some redefinition of the goals of the institutions. They are *college preparatory* schools, and a change in goals would make them something different.

Another area of discrepancy involved students' individuality. All groups seemed to feel that the schools should place much more emphasis than they do on helping students discover and fulfill themselves as persons, helping students develop their characters, and helping students become intellectually independent. These goals are related to another goal, which students felt was given too much emphasis, molding students according to society's expectations. The underlying message in these results seems to reflect, once again, the rather one-sided press of the schools for academic excellence. Oddly, there seems to be a desire for a focus on ethical development—not necessarily the traditional approach of preaching conservative moral ideas to students, but rather an approach which emphasizes personal choices and individual growth toward personal standards for living. One possible guide for the schools which wished to accomplish this change in goals lies in the work of Kohlberg (1970), who suggests some ways that the schools could help students find and develop their ideas for living. Kohlberg's research has been based on the idea that moral thinking progresses through levels he terms preconventional, conventional, and postconventional. The person at the preconventional level thinks in terms of good and bad, interpreting these labels in terms of their physical consequences, such as punishments, rewards, and exchanges of favors, or in terms of the power of those who provide the rules and label actions as good or bad. The person at the conventional level conforms to the expectations and rules of his or her family, group and nation. The conventional thinker believes these expectations and the social order that they represent are valuable in their own right and deserve to be maintained, supported, and justified. Many parents, teachers, and administrators believe that the schools should emphasize these conventional views. The person at the postconventional level seeks moral principles that are valid for, and apply to everyone, regardless of the authority (or lack of authority) of the persons who hold them. The postconventional level is further divided into two stages: the social contract orientation and the universal ethical principle orientation. In the social contract stage, the right action is one that is based on general standards and rights that have been agreed upon by the whole society, while recognizing that personal values and opinions are relative. Open and free agreement and contracts are the basis of obligations. In the universal ethical principle stage, the right action is a result of deciding on the basis of conscience in terms of self-chosen ethical principles. These principles involve justice, the equality and reciprocity of human rights and respect for the dignity of human beings as individuals.

According to Kohlberg, moral development passes naturally through these stages. Moral education consists of helping the person reach the next step of development in his or her moral thinking, rather than teaching an official or conventional doctrine. The goal of moral education, then, is to increase the student's ability to make moral judgments on his or her own, rather than to conform to the ideas of teachers or adults. To reach this goal, Kohlberg suggests that teachers encourage students to confront genuine moral conflicts, examine the kind of reasoning they use to think about the conflicts, try to see the inadequacies and inconsistencies in their thinking, and find ways to resolve the inadequacies and inconsistencies. Kohlberg believes these steps could be part of regular class work in such areas as social studies, literature, and sex education. The evidence from Kohlberg's studies suggests that the results of working moral education into the curriculum are well worth the effort. The elite schools could probably perform this task well, if they chose to do so.

A related area, affective education, is another aspect of individual development that could be worked into the schools. Various experimental projects have attempted to deal directly with students' feelings. Although most of these programs are still in the experimental stage, they seem to have had some successes. The programs are designed to help students recognize and identify their feelings, verbalize them, analyze them, and deal with them in rational ways.

Yet another tool for personal development is aesthetic education. The schools could increase their courses and extracurricular activities which would encourage students to express their perceptions and feelings in plastic and verbal forms. Helping students to develop their own styles of expression, and to communicate their subjective and private views of the world would surely help them become more complete persons.

What of the Future?

Perhaps the most important question about the philosophy of the schools is how they can organize their programs to be relevant to the ethical and moral problems their students will face in their lives. The answers to this question are difficult ones, which stem from the rapidly changing nature of our society, and they have no simple solutions because of the speed and complexity of the changes. However, observers have begun to see some of the outlines of the society of the future and the ethical changes upon which that society will be based. Jean-Francois Revel (1974), for example, has described a group of interrelated changes that present challenges to our schools and other social institutions. The first, and most general, change is a radically new approach to moral values, allowing and encouraging a greater openness to experiences. The emphasis is on variety, novelty, complexity, and autonomy. Few experiences are ruled out if they add to the breadth and complexity of a person's personality. In response to this change, the schools could follow the suggestions made in the last few pages. They could also offer more courses on a variety of topics, and could broaden the definitions of what constitutes credit. However, there are limits to what the schools can do. They are limited by their own traditional roles and values, as well as by the expectations of parents. For example, a course in human sexuality could not be offered at many schools today, and at most of the schools which would offer such a course, the discussions would probably be very intellectualized. The schools are devoted to an academic and intellectual approach to all subjects, so the schools may find it difficult to adapt to their students' desires for a greater variety of emotions, intuitions, feelings, thoughts, and perceptions. However, some of the social and community action programs may provide some of these experiences.

The second change described by Revel is the black and other minority revolutions which forcefully bring the latent racism of many aspects of our society to mind. The elite schools seem to be having no worse and, in some ways, a little better success in this area than many social institutions. There are still a very few schools which exclude minority students, but this is mostly done inadvertently. The "A Better Chance" program has actively recruited minority students for independent schools. In this area the schools seem to have made a serious effort. However, in the broad area of making students aware of their own attitudes and dealing constructively with the problems of intergroup relations, the elite schools have had no greater success than the rest of our society.

The third change is the acceptance of guilt for poverty. It may be ironic that the feeling of responsibility for the "forgotten Americans," in Michael Harrington's phrase, is probably stronger in the elite schools than in the typical suburban middle class school. It seems strange to hear students in the elite schools talk about tearing down the corrupt capitalistic system, and working for an equalitarian Socialist society, when many of them come from families which are the backbone of American industrialism. Beyond intensifying the community work they already provide, and courses in the economics of American society, which they could easily provide, it is hard to see what actions the schools could take to help their students answer the question of who is responsible for the wide spread poverty and economic inequality in our society.

The next change is a logical extension of the last: the growing demand for equality in all spheres, including the classroom. It is ironic that the institutions which the society charges with teaching democracy are so undemocratic. Of course, most Americans spend their lives in undemocratic institutions, such as large businesses, government agencies, and other bureaucratic organizations, in which the procedure is the line of command, not the free election and discussion of issues. However, much more could be done to break down the artificial barriers of status and privilege in the schools. It would not be an easy task in the best of circumstances, let alone in schools which have been organized on hierarchical principles for a century or more. Teachers and administrators are unlikely to wish to give up their positions of authority, and there may be good reasons to question whether they should. This is a fundamental philosophical division of opinion, and the question of the extent of student-teacher equality may be one of the most difficult for the schools to deal with in the future.

One aspect of equality which the schools are meeting with no better success than the rest of society is the feminist challenge to masculine domination. The schools have approached coeducation with considerable caution, although single sex schools are not necessarily based on sexist beliefs. However, single sex schools probably make it harder to change such beliefs among students. (Several commentators have made a case for single sex schools, particularly girls' schools, as allowing the sexes to develop in their own ways, but they do not present very much convincing evidence.) The faculty salary statistics sometimes reveal discrimination against women in the elite schools, and the attitudes upon which the salaries are based may be subtly exhibited throughout the school. In any case, most schools are not actively trying to help their students come to terms with the intricacies of the new equality of the sexes.

A more pervasive change is the young's rejection of exclusively economic and technological social goals. Again, it is ironic that this sentiment is particularly strong among the elite school students, since many come from families which are strongly committed to these goals. Competition, materialism, and personal success are increasingly suspect among some students. Many believe that competition has led to a lack of community in America, the neglect of the poor, a refusal to take responsibility for the ills of society, and control of political power by private interests. In their view, materialism has led to uncontrolled technology, and the destruction of the environment, and the desire for personal success has led to a willingness to manipulate others for one's own ends, artificiality to the point of dishonesty in work and culture, and a concern only for one's family. These sentiments are not held by all students, of course, but they are widely discussed in many schools in bull sessions after class. Some schools have brought some of the discussions into the classroom, but few have made any concerted effort to do so.

The next change may present some problems to the schools: the rejection of an authoritarian culture in favor of a critical and diversified culture. Most Americans work and live in bureaucratic organizations based on authority. The expression of opinions and feelings have prescribed limits. One traditional role of the schools and colleges was to prepare students for places in the organizations of the society. Most schools still do not examine our social institutions of business, industry, and government very closely. They are themselves built on a conception of the teacher and the taught as the knowledgeable speaker and the uninformed listener. The encouragement of criticism and free expression is hard to deal with in educational, as well as other settings. However, many of the schools seem to be making efforts in this direction.

The rejection of the spread of American power abroad and criticisms of an expansive foreign policy are easier to discuss in the schools. Although they are not part of the regular curriculum in most schools the criticisms are part of the intellectual atmosphere at most schools. Certainly, the old ideas of "country, right or wrong," are scarcely to be seen except among some of the older faculty.

Finally, the schools are able to accept the determination that the natural environment is more important than commercial profit. The schools have provided courses, projects, readings, and time for the study and implementation of ecological principles.

In sum, the elite schools seem to have had mixed success in dealing with the ethical problems of a rapidly changing and confusing society. Their own traditions both limit and help their efforts. Some in the schools want their schools to be defenders of traditional values, to the point of being blind to the realities of change. However, many schools are committed to a rational discussion of options and the responsibilities they entail, a tradition which may be their best guarantee that they will be relevant to the ethical problems their students will face.

7

The Consequences of the Elite Schools for Their Students

The ultimate criterion of the success of the elite schools lies in their impact on their students. This criterion extends far beyond the placement of students in prestigious colleges, and includes students' personal development, growth in social skills, changes in moral and ethical ideas, and increases in self-discipline. In this study, we tried to assess the impact of the schools on students in three ways. The first approach was to consider the immediate effects of the schools which result from their day-to-day operations—the stresses the schools create in students. The second approach was to study the consequences of the schools for students' development based on students' reports of their own feelings about the influence of the schools on their lives. The third approach is based on a more objective assessment of the impact of the schools on students. The views of entering students who were new to the schools were compared to the views of senior and junior students who had been in the schools for several years. The comparisons of their views of themselves, their schools, and their own development lead to some enlightening conclusions about the nature of the elite schools.

Stresses on Students

People have recognized for years that adolescence is a time of stress, but research showing that educational institutions may have built-in features that cause stress is relatively recent. These studies have shown that many schools encourage competition and place heavy study loads on students; others place ambiguous or conflicting demands on them. At the same time, students are involved in extracurricular activities and roles that place difficult demands on their time and energy. Other students feel that the school is irrelevant and they feel out of place in it. In addition, there are the traditional interpersonal stresses of adolescence relating to parents, peers, and the opposite sex. Further, many students face difficult personal problems in developing a viable moral code, determining their religious beliefs, and gaining a personal sense of identity. There are the practical career problems of deciding whether to go to work or go to college and then the problems of actually getting a job or getting into a college. Finally, many elite school students are concerned with racial and ethnic relations and national and world problems.

In our study we designed a question to assess the degree to which students are bothered by such potential sources of stress. Even though some of them are beyond the school's control, it is important to know how students feel about them.

The question, shown in Table 7-1, asked students to indicate the extent to which they were bothered by thirteen potential sources of stress. Teachers and administrators were asked to indicate the extent to which they felt students were bothered by the same sources. The four sources that students reported bothered them *most* were first, national or world problems; second, pressures for grades; third, relations between racial and ethnic groups; and fourth, school rules and regulations. The three sources that students reported bothered them *least* were deciding what to do after high school graduation, being "in" or "out" with certain groups of students, and deciding about religious beliefs. Students appeared to be most concerned about the great issues of the times, their own academic performance, and the constrictive rules of their schools. Since nearly

Table 7-1

Pressures on Students

(in percentages)

Area of Pressure	Group								
	Students			Teachers			Administrators		
	N*	L	V	N	L	V	N	L	V
Pressures for grades	15	37	45	2	30	63	1	33	60
Difficulty of classwork	33	48	16	6	66	23	6	68	20
School rules and regulations	22	32	43	7	41	47	5	41	50
Being "in" or "out" with certain groups of students	57	29	9	10	43	32	11	45	32
Concern about getting into college	38	27	31	1	15	79	0	20	74
Relations with the opposite sex	31	40	25	4	52	25	4	55	27
Deciding what to do after high school graduation	58	23	14	38	38	14	35	41	15
Pressures from parents	40	36	21	3	53	35	1	49	41
Deciding what is right in moral questions	40	36	18	11	54	20	8	56	28
National or world problems	6	29	60	4	40	52	4	35	56
Relations between racial and ethnic groups	15	34	44	11	55	27	6	58	29
Deciding about religious beliefs	53	26	16	30	47	8	33	48	10
Gaining a sense of personal identity	25	35	36	3	29	60	3	23	68

Source: *Questionnaire for Students, Teachers and Administrators* and *Questionnaire for New Students,* Educational Testing Service and the Secondary School Research Program, © 1971, 1972, Educational Testing Service.

*N = Not bothered at all; L = Bothered a little; V = Bothered very much; Not shown = "Can't say" or no response

The item read as follows:

Students–To what extent are you bothered by the following at the present time?

Teachers and administrators–To what extent do you feel students are bothered by the following at the present time?

all the students in the sample planned to go to college, they were probably not concerned about what to do after high school. The lack of concern about being "in" or "out" may indicate that the day of the clique is over in most independent schools, as we saw in the chapters on student life. The lack of concern about religious belief suggested in this question reinforces the results in the last chapter that suggested that most independent school students do not strongly value traditional religion.

Teachers and administrators generally thought students were more bothered than the students reported they were in virtually every area. The discrepancy between the stress attributed to students and the stress they actually report is particularly striking in several areas. Teachers and administrators thought students would be more concerned than they were with popularity with certain groups of students, pressures from parents, gaining a sense of identity, and, most strikingly, concern about getting into college. Perhaps students are more realistic about getting into college than teachers and administrators. Especially in these times of open admissions, there is a college for students of virtually any level of ability.

It is striking that students were not bothered by many things which are supposed to bother them in the popular view. For example, the need to decide what is morally right, and deciding about religious beliefs bothered few students very much. Although there are probably a few students who agonize over ethical and religious beliefs, the average student does not seem particularly bothered by these choices.

Finally, as we noted in the chapter on student groups, some commentators feel that the adolescent peer group holds a tyrannical sway over today's students. We have found that the students were bothered less from worries of "being in or out with certain groups of students" than any other potential source of stress. In sum, we have little evidence to support some of the ideas about causes for adolescent turmoil and agitation. These ideas generally place the causes within the student. Perhaps these ideas are popular because they avoid the possibility that the causes of student stress are, in large measure, due to the schools and our other social institutions. Adults need to accept the idea that much adolescent turmoil is their responsibility, not something students will grow out of.

These ideas are supported by the responses to a related question shown in Table 7-2, in which students were asked to indicate their degree of satisfaction with their development in eighteen areas, covering traits that are important aspects of the transition from adolescence to adulthood. The majority of students were satisfied with their development in every area. They were particularly satisfied in seven areas (over 75 percent indicated they were satisfied or strongly satisfied). These areas were physical growth, general health, ability to get along with members of their own sex, ability to get along with adults other than their parents, physical appearance, self-reliance, and ability to make ethical

Table 7-2
Students' Satisfaction with Their Personal Development
(in percentages)

Area of Development	Degree of Satisfaction		
	D*	S	SS
Physical growth	17	64	12
Ability to relate to the opposite sex	31	48	15
General health	7	56	34
Ability to handle tension	22	51	21
Physical appearance	14	67	13
Ability to control emotions	21	55	19
Ability to remain happy most of the time	26	46	21
Ability to compete without resenting competitors	19	52	21
Ability to keep going when feelings are hurt	24	52	18
Self-reliance	16	48	31
Ability to stick to a task	28	46	20
Knowing my own abilities	22	54	18
Ability to get along with parents	21	41	33
Ability to get along with other adults	9	50	36
Ability to get along with members of my own sex	8	60	28
Ability to make ethical or moral distinctions	10	55	24
Developing a philosophy of life	25	44	20
Developing a clear sense of myself (who I am)	29	42	20

Source: *Questionnaire for Students, Teachers and Administrators* and *Questionnaire for New Students*, Educational Testing Service and the Secondary School Research Program, © 1971, 1972, Educational Testing Service.
*D = Strongly dissatisfied *or* Dissatisfied; S = Satisfied; SS = Strongly Satisfied; Not shown = Can't say and no response
The item read as follows: (Students only) How satisfied are you with your personal development in the following areas?

or moral decisions. Few students were dissatisfied with themselves. In fact, in only five areas did as many as a quarter of the students indicate they were dissatisfied or strongly dissatisfied. These areas were developing a clear sense of themselves, ability to relate to the opposite sex, ability to stick to a task, ability to remain happy most of the time, and developing a philosophy of life. Altogether, these self-evaluations suggest that the students in the study had a high level of maturity and confidence. Although some students expressed dissatisfaction in some areas, the general picture is one of realistic, adaptable and responsible youth who are ready to move on to college and adulthood. Thus, the pressures they reported would not seem to be primarily of their own making, but due to their situation.

The question of pressures on students elicited a good deal of comment. One teacher pointed out that students feel many kinds of pressures.

"Students" are bothered by various pressures: there are some students in all categories for each kind of pressure. At this school the pressure of the burden of classwork and of the concern about college entrance are probably the most severe along with the strong personal pressure to achieve identity that is usual in adolescence. The pressure to get along with the opposite sex is, of course, always strong.

Other people were skeptical about the "pressures" students feel.

There are those who feel little pressure from their studies as they could care less yet show a concern, though only superficial sometimes, with our society and its problems. I believe our more mature students are the ones who excel and do have genuine feeling of pressure from grades, etc., and present social problems. Often deficient students write off poor grades with the excuse that they are overcome by social problems.

What Can Be Done?

Although the school cannot realistically affect all of the sources of stress we studied, it can help students cope with them. Some of the possibilities are discussion groups, counseling, suggested readings, and course assignments. The sources of stress within the school may be more directly approached by considering changes in certain areas of school life. The results in the other areas we have examined offer specific suggestions.

The results of our survey make clear some of the psychological costs of the schools' current programs and purposes. Since the schools strongly stress academic accomplishment and are strongly oriented toward the college-going student, one of the costs may be student stress due to pressures for grades, difficulty of class work, or concern about college entry. The schools could do some things to lessen pressures from these sources. And even if the source of stress is outside the school, knowledge of these pressures could encourage an appreciation by teachers and administrators of the stresses on students.

One area may be particularly difficult for the schools to alter—the sizable minority of students who are searching for a firm sense of themselves. We found that 36 percent of the students said they were bothered very much by the pressures of gaining a sense of personal identity, and 35 percent said they were bothered a little. We then found that 29 percent were dissatisfied or strongly dissatisfied with their development of a clear sense of who they were, the area of second greatest dissatisfaction. These results may be related to the fact that the schools offer identity chiefly in terms of academic accomplishment. The schools need to find ways to assure students that they are more than grades and test scores. Some schools do have many nonacademic programs which are challenging and help the students learn that they are good at more things than classwork. However, unless the schools are willing to lessen their pressures for academic achievement, the schools can probably do little to help students find themselves, except to make available interested and sympathetic adults who can help the students work through their doubts and uncertainties. We shall return to this subject in the final chapter.

Impact of the Schools on the Students: Comparing
Ninth Graders with Seniors

As a reader looks through the catalogues of the elite schools or their descriptions of themselves in the *Independent Secondary Schools: A Handbook* (1971), one finds such glowing descriptions of the benefits of attending the schools as these:

. . . admission to college is not the exclusive objective. Our purpose is to expose each student to a broad variety of academic courses and experiences undiminished by narrow or premature specialization.

_____ strives to stimulate clear thinking, to establish the highest ideals, to encourage a broad outlook on life, and to develop in each boy the sense of purpose and responsibility so necessary for leadership.

The entire program is based on a firm belief that the well-being of mankind depends upon each person's willingness and ability to become informed about and to act upon issues confronting our world. The complete educational experience at _____ prepares boys to take their responsible place in society by creating in them an awareness of the issues, building concern, developing competence, and encouraging a commitment to action while at school and in later life.

Most of the administrators in the schools firmly believe that their schools do these things, and, as we have seen, so do many faculty members and students, although they may express doubts about certain of them. Parents, as Kraushaar's report (1972) has shown, place heavy weight on the presumed benefits of the independent school experience. All of these people are expressing a special variety of the fundamental American belief in the wondrous powers of schools to mold and change students.

Generations of Americans have been taught to revere education. The more education the better; the better the schools, the better the education; the more and better the education, the better the subsequent life of the student. This belief was called into question by the results of the Coleman Report, and was more recently sharply attacked by the sociologist Christopher Jencks and his Harvard colleagues (1972). Once they took into consideration the effects of ability and family background these researchers found little evidence to show that the schools have a large influence on an individual's later income or accomplishments. (Similar research on the impact of college can be summarized briefly: colleges differ very little in their influence on students, once students' backgrounds and ability are controlled. Going to college has a relatively small impact on students' values or accomplishments, once their initial abilities and attitudes are taken into account.) There is some professional dispute about the size of the impacts of schools and colleges, but it is clear that research has not shown education to have an effect anything like that most people believe it has.

As said at the outset, most of the people who work in independent schools believe their schools have pervasive and powerful effects on students. And this seems to be a logical belief when we consider the intensity and direction of the elite schools' environments. If any schools could change students it would be these. They try to move their students up to high levels of academic competence. They strive to give them "character" and "principles." Is there any evidence that this effort does, in fact, change the students?

Our study did not follow a group of students through four years of school as would be required to study their change in a way that would meet the technical and statistical requirements of a study of the impact of the schools. However, we did ask the same or similar questions of the entering students and the older students. By comparing the answers of the two groups of students we can get some idea of the direction and size of the impact of the schools on their students.

Let us begin with a simple piece of information—the highest amount of education the students hope to attain. Among the entering students, about 86 percent planned to graduate from a four-year college, compared to 90 percent of the older students. About 47 percent of the entering students planned some degree requiring work beyond the bachelor's compared to 55 percent of the older students. Thus, while the older students' ambitions were slightly higher, the students entering the schools came with very high aspirations and it would appear that the school had—and could only have—a very small impact on them.

But what about the more important areas of values, goals for living, and self-confidence? Doesn't the elite school experience influence them? Again, it is not possible to give a technically final answer to that question, but we do have some data. The same item on values described in Chapter 6 was asked of new students as well as the older students. The students were asked to choose the three values they felt were closest to their own views from a list of thirteen statements of values. Among the new students only three values were endorsed by as many as a third of the students: "Standing up for your own rights" (chosen by 51 percent), "being independent and original" (49 percent), and "being friendly to people even if they do things against your own beliefs" (36 percent). In Chapter 6 we found that the same three values were chosen most frequently by the older students—the comparable figures being 52, 64, and 37 percent, respectively. Three values were chosen by fewer than 10 percent of the new students: "demanding and getting the respect you deserve," "being poised, gracious and charming no matter where you are," and "living your religion in your daily life." The first two values were also endorsed by less than 10 percent of the older students, and the last by only 15 percent. The only value on which there was any sizable difference was "working hard to achieve academic honors," but the direction of the difference would not encourage many teachers—32 percent of the new students endorse this value in contrast to 13 percent of older students. Thus, if we accept the validity of these figures, there is no compelling evidence that the schools influence students' values very much at all, except perhaps to value independence more and academic attainment less.

Both new and old students were also asked the questions on life goals that were described in Chapter 6. Due to the difficulty of the language level and the misunderstanding shown in some pilot surveys, some of the life goal items were rewritten or deleted. However, some could be compared. The comparable goals, and the percentage of each group considering them very important or essential, were as follows: "find personal happiness" 86 percent of the new students, 89 percent of the old; "have a happy family life," 82 percent and 79 percent; "be of service to others," 57 percent and 65 percent; "change the world for the better," 51 percent and 54 percent; "be a scholar, teacher, scientist, etc.," 26 percent and 30 percent; "make a lot of money," 30 percent and 24 percent; and "be active in politics," 12 percent and 7 percent. The differences between the new and old students are minor, and, more important, the general profile of life goals is the same. Both new and old students valued their own happiness highest; then helping others. Money and political position had little appeal to most new and old students. (Kraushaar has pointed out that financial success may mean less to students who have never been in want themselves and who have not seen their families struggle to attain middle class respectability.)

The elite schools seem to have little influence on the long-term goals of their students. At this point someone might object that the influence of the school may not be reflected in this value or that goal, but that the real power of the schools to influence students lies in their people and programs. The schools may not have a direct influence on values or goals according to this view, but the schools should help students develop their own ideas. Again, our results do not allow us to respond to this idea in a completely satisfactory way, but we can provide some data which reflect on it, by examining the sources of students' values. New students were asked to indicate how much their outlook on life was influenced by twelve possible sources of values, such as parents, films and TV, etc. This was a slight modification of the question asked of old students that was described in Chapter 6. The old students were asked to indicate only the most important sources of their values. Only two sources were acknowledged as having "a lot" of influence by a majority of new students: "my own thinking" and "parents." The only two sources considered important by older students were "parents" and "student friends." "Reading" was a fairly important source to both groups of students. New and old students agreed that several sources of values were unimportant: school counselors, school courses in religion or ethics, other school courses, community service, and clergymen, priests, or rabbis. Teachers were said to have a lot of influence by 29 percent of the new students; they were described as important sources of values by 21 percent of the old students. Thus, the formal efforts of the schools to influence students' values had a minor overall impact, and did not gain strength while the students stayed in the schools. The influence of teachers was relatively minor; over time their influence seems—if moving in any direction—to decline. The only sizable difference was that the old students seemed to give more attention to other students than new students. Again, there is no strong evidence that the schools have an important impact on the values of students.

We now turn to an area even harder to assess than values—the students' sense of themselves. New students were asked a slightly modified version of the item on their satisfaction with their personal characteristics that was described earlier in this chapter. The great majority of both new and old students were satisfied with themselves in most areas, and to about the same extent. Two-thirds or more in both groups were satisfied with their ability to get along with friends of their own sex, health, ability to tell right from wrong, ability to get along with their parents, appearance, and ability to be happy most of the time. Older students were more satisfied with themselves than new students in five areas: ability to compete without being jealous of others who do well, ability to keep going when one's feelings are hurt, ability to stick to a job, knowledge of one's own abilities, and ability to handle worries. Thus, old students expressed more satisfaction with their persistence, stability, control of their emotions, and self-insight. This cluster of traits seems to reflect the greater general maturity of the older students. It is hard to say how much of this difference is due to the schools and how much is due to students' general maturation. However, it is the first evidence that the school may have an influence on important student characteristics.

Now, instead of comparing the responses of new and old students to the surveys, let us see what the old students said about their progress when we asked them to describe the influence of the school on their lives. We asked older students to describe the extent to which their schools had affected their standing on the outcomes of secondary education. The question we used needed to be formulated very carefully since secondary education affects many aspects of students' lives including their skills, knowledge, maturity, and attitudes. Because of the multiplicity of such effects, it is difficult to specify outcomes of secondary education that will be broad enough to include the major effects and narrow enough to be meaningful. One useful way of studying the outcomes is to consider the developmental tasks faced by secondary school students. Developmental tasks are:

... skills, knowledge, functions, and attitudes which an individual has to acquire at a certain point in his life; they are acquired through physical maturation, social expectations, and personal efforts. Successful mastery of these tasks will result in adjustment ... and will prepare the individual for the harder tasks ahead. Failure in a given developmental task will result in a corresponding lack of adjustment, increased anxiety, social disapproval, and the inability to handle the more difficult tasks to come. ... Through its socializing agents and methods of reinforcement and punishment, society attempts to help the individual learn those developmental tasks at their proper age levels" (Muuss, 1966).

As one of the socializing agents for society, the school attempts to help students master the developmental tasks of late adolescence, so that they may go on to the tasks of young adulthood. After examining the psychological literature on adolescence and reviewing the tasks with groups of teachers, administrators, and students, the project staff developed the list of sixteen tasks, shown in Table 7-3. Some of these have clear educational implications, such as the ability to think and reason; some are by-products of schooling, such as the ability to follow through with a project or interest; and some have only a slight relation to the school's efforts, such as getting along well with one's parents; but all are tasks that adolescents must master, either during school or in the years immediately following it. Since our purpose was to gain information about the impact of the schools on students, the questions asked students to describe their school's influence on their progress in these areas. They could indicate whether they felt their school had hindered their progress, neither hindered nor helped, helped their progress a little, or helped their progress a great deal.

A statistical analysis of the responses of older students was quite revealing. The correlations showed that several traits seem to be central, in the sense that they are related to several other traits. Improving one's ability to work with people who are different from oneself was related to improving one's self-confidence (.48),[a] becoming psychologically independent of one's parents (.40), improving one's sense of responsibility (.47), improving one's ability to think and reason (.43), and understanding people who differ from oneself in racial or ethnic background (.48). This might be termed an *interpersonal maturity* cluster.

Improving one's sense of responsibility was related to becoming psychologically independent of one's parents (.41), improving one's ability to work with people different from oneself (.47), being independent of the opinions of other students (.44), improving one's ability to think and reason (.59), increasing one's

[a]These numbers are correlations, statistics which indicate the relationship between two variables. If two variables are perfectly related, the correlation would be 1.00; if they had no relation, it would be .00.

Table 7-3
Students' Sense of Progress
(in percentages)

Area of Concern	Sense of Progress		
	H*	N	HE
Knowing about jobs and work after graduation	13	68	15
Becoming politically aware	11	22	63
Developing skills useful for many kinds of jobs	18	44	33
Improving my self-confidence	18	22	56
Improving my ability to work with people who are different from me	8	22	65
Helping me appreciate art, music, and other artistic work	10	33	54
Becoming psychologically independent of my parents	4	33	59
Preparing for marriage and children	18	60	16
Being independent of the opinions of other students	11	38	45
Improving my sense of responsibility	7	21	67
Improving my ability to think and reason	5	11	79
Increasing my desire to learn	13	20	63
Understanding people who differ from me in racial or ethnic background	10	31	53
Learning how to make better ethical or moral distinctions	9	46	40
Getting along well with my parents	11	61	23
Developing my ability to follow through with a project, interest, or task	9	29	57

Source: *Questionnaire for Students, Teachers and Administrators* and *Questionnaire for New Students*, Educational Testing Service and the Secondary School Research Program, © 1971, 1972, Educational Testing Service.
*H = Hindered my progress; N = Neither hindered nor helped; HE = Helped my progress a little *or* Helped my progress a great deal
The item read as follows: (Students only) Do you think your school has hindered or helped your progress in each of the following areas?

desire to learn (.45), learning how to make better ethical and moral distinctions (.40), and developing one's ability to follow through with a project, interest, or task (.51). This might be termed a *personal maturity* cluster.

Improving one's ability to think and reason, related to the two central traits above, was also related to increasing one's desire to learn (.56) and developing one's ability to follow through with a project, interest, or task (.51). This might be termed a *task-orientation maturity* cluster.

Each of these maturity clusters had connections with the others; each cluster seems to show one aspect of general maturity. That they are not all highly correlated indicates the complexity and multifaceted nature of maturity and development.

The results show that the majority of students felt their school had helped their progress a little or a great deal in ten areas: becoming politically aware; improving their self-confidence; improving their ability to work with people who are different from themselves; helping them appreciate art, music, and other artistic work; becoming psychologically independent of their parents; improving their sense of responsibility; improving their ability to think and reason; increasing their desire to learn; understanding people who differ from them in racial or ethnic backgrounds; and developing their ability to follow through with a project, interest, or task. Most of these have educational implications. In contrast, the majority of students thought their school had neither hindered nor helped their progress in three areas: knowing about jobs and work after graduation, preparing for marriage and children, and getting along well with parents. In addition, the majority of students said their school had either hindered their progress or neither hindered nor helped in three other areas: developing skills useful for many kinds of jobs, being independent of the opinions of other students, and learning how to make better ethical or moral distinctions. These results suggest that students felt their schools had helped them in a number of areas directly related to the academic curriculum and other areas related to the indirect effects of the school setting. That is, improving students' ability to think and reason, increasing their desire to learn, and even helping them to become politically aware are related to the academic emphasis and curricula of these schools. Further, classwork, extracurricular activities, and the need to meet various deadlines in school probably help students develop a sense of responsibility, learn to work with people who differ from them, and learn to follow through with a project, interest, or task. And perhaps when students successfully complete these various roles on their own, in their own right as individuals, they also gain a sense of responsibility and gradually feel independent from their parents. Of course the intellectual power students gain as they study their subjects must also contribute to a sense of independence from parents.

The areas in which students felt no influence or a negative influence from the school are typically simply not part of the concerns of most of these schools. These schools are primarily academic institutions that are unconcerned about such things as work and marriage, although they claim to be concerned with the independence of their students. Of course, this lack of concern may disturb some people. As one student commented:

I feel that this question is quite eye-opening. Those answers that I marked "help my progress a little" were few and far between, and in only one case did school help me a great deal. The question I ask myself, then, is what is the relevancy of school? It didn't help me in any of these areas which I think are very important in day-to-day living.

In interpreting these results, it is well to recall the considerations bearing on the schools' goals as described in Chapter 6. For example, the adults in most schools probably hope they help students learn to make better ethical and moral distinctions. But not all schools would feel that way. And this is the crux of the problem. Whether the schools would be satisfied with the results depends on their goals and purposes. For example, if they feel that helping students prepare for such difficult adult roles as being marriage partners and parents is irrelevant to the school or if they feel that helping students make ethical distinctions are not part of the purposes of their school, then they will not be disturbed if students feel they have not made progress in these areas. If they feel that learning to appreciate art, music, and other forms of aesthetic activity is important, they will be concerned if students feel they have not made progress in these areas. Overall, most of the elite schools probably would feel that many of their goals are being met, as indicated in the students' responses, but that there are several areas where they probably would feel that they need to make a better effort.

The schools' ability to affect students may be limited, however, since many students are already fairly mature by the time they reach ninth grade. As one student put it, referring to the questions just described, "In most of these areas, my ideas and values were already formulated by the time I entered this school. The impact of this school had not affected me as much as the political and social changes that take place in the world around us." Schools may also feel they are affecting students, when the changes are actually due to maturation. One student, recognizing the difficulty, expressed ". . . doubt about whether psychological and intellectual changes happen in the school's atmosphere, or *because* of it," and another pointed out, ". . . it is possible that a person may progress in some of these fields by merely maturing while in high school. The high school years are those in which a person does mature the most" Another student raised a related point, the importance of individual effort:

I have found that any changes I have undergone while at school are not the work of the school itself; they are the result of thought on my part, this thought having been stimulated by simply being here. . . . Possibly the school can take credit for putting a student in a situation requiring thought, but it is the student who makes the difference, by his reaction to the situation, and, ironically, such thought producing situations are often those least expected to be, while planned situations most often do not produce the wanted result.

Several students wrote of the impact of their schools and the goals they would like their schools to pursue. For example, one student spoke for many when he wrote: "The basic problem with school is that it doesn't prepare young people with the basic background necessary for going out and facing the world as it *is*. Changes have been made in this direction, but more are needed." Another student emphasized that the effects of isolation and insulation from society might be the opposite from those the school assumes they will have:

This school prepares one for college as far as work is concerned; however, it does not prepare one socially. Here one is inhibited and almost has a nervous breakdown when one goes home on a weekend. Getting into college is deified.... When girls leave this boarding school, they go wild. The freedom they have been waiting for in the last 3 years surges forth. They feel that they must do everything they have been restrained from doing. No longer is the little housemother telling you when to make your bed or go to bed.... When we finally get out of here, we will be intellectual book computers but will not be able to intelligently conduct ourselves in the big outside world from which in the last years we have been sheltered.

Another student made a related point:

I feel schools should be more involved with giving students a total education. Today people must learn how to live in the environment and with fellow man. School should be concerned more with education than with discipline. True, people who are a disruptive influence should be taught to contribute rather than detract from the school, but the disciplining for minor offenses is ridiculous. Schools should survive problems and educate unbiasedly those they would kick out and ignore. A school is for education, not just containing people.

Another related major theme was that the school should try to educate the total person. One student commented (along with illustrative drawings): "I am an individual, and want to be treated like one—this school educates heads, not emotions. Living = learning (or should)." Another student expressed the same idea:

I'm not sure that my school develops individuals to their very fullest extent, but I am also not sure that this would be possible in the type of school in which I am enrolled (college prep). The emphasis here is getting into college, and developing a strong sense of comradeship, competitiveness, moral standards (a little strict perhaps), and basically getting along with people in future life. It is not a terribly creative school, but then as I said I'm not sure it could be, and remain the same school it is. I must also say that sometimes the lack of females here is a deterrent to certain values.

Another student also sought broader education:

The most important thing in school is to develop socially and internally. The student should be helped to be friendly and outgoing as well as standing up for his rights. At this level too much emphasis is put on grades, for the student is developing at a rapid rate, and he should be able to handle himself with his friends. In line with this, more emphasis should be put on sex education. I think that concentrating on social problems would help rather than hinder the students ability and desire to learn.

The increased breadth should also include a breadth of goals in the view of many students: "Character, leadership, concern for others are not something the faculty can instill in students. It must come from the individual and should not necessarily have to meet a prefabricated standard of what is good."

Finally, one student pointed out that the purposes of the school related to the purposes of society:

Today, it seems that the educational system of this country does not create the most aware person as possible. I say this because of the tremendous amount of apathy and indifference that plagues our nation. When it takes an assassination like King's or Kennedy's, to create interest in the country, something must be corrected. The most probable place to start this correction is in the educational system, because it is most likely that the school carries the intrinsic values that dominate our life. Perhaps if we changed our educational system, then our priorities as a nation and as a people might be changed.

These comments support the results of the statistical analyses. The students seem to be saying that the schools have had little impact on some significant areas of their lives. They recognize that they have received good academic educations, but they are fully aware of the cost to their development in other areas, and recognize the stresses the school creates in their lives, as we found earlier in this chapter.

By and large the students seem to *feel* they have made progress during their years in the elite schools, although we have little evidence that they have changed. (We should point out that this lack of evidence is partly due to the fact that many of the areas in which students feel they have made progress are not covered in other questions.) Students feel they have become more confident, responsible, independent, rational, interested in learning, and appreciative of art. They also feel they have become better able to work with others, and that they understand the political system. The statistical evidence, as well as the comments of students suggests that students' growth is due less to the deliberate programs of the schools than to the students' contact with other students, informal conversations with teachers, activities outside the classroom, reading in the library, and the school's general emphasis on ideas and their consequences. The elite schools do seem to have an impact on their students, but the schools' power to influence their students' development seems to depend more on their general atmospheres than their specific academic programs. In the next chapter we shall compare the sense of progress felt by the elite school students with that felt by public school students, after which we shall examine the question of the changing impact of elite schools on their students.

8

The Value of an Elite School Education: Comparisons with the Public School Alternative

Why should a family spend $5,000 a year or more to send a child to an independent school? Over a period of four years, a family could provide a child with some exceptional educational experiences with $20,000. For example, they could send their child to Europe, travel through America, give him or her individual music lessons, buy a library of books, or set up a laboratory in their home, to mention a few of the possibilities. Why, then, should they choose an independent school? The answers usually given to this question primarily reflect a belief in the academic superiority of the schools. For example, the majority of parents of independent school students surveyed by Kraushaar (1972) cited five reasons for their choice of school: smaller classes, better teachers, better training in diligence and study habits, more academically challenging curriculum, and greater likelihood of admission to a college of their choice. In one way or another, these reasons are based on the assumption that the independent school student will emerge from that experience with a better academic preparation than if he or she had gone to a public school.

Another belief, widely held by the staffs of independent schools, is that the schools provide a better environment than the public schools for moral growth. The catalogue statements quoted in the last chapter reflect this belief. Many school people hold a similar faith in the power of their schools to help students develop their personalities in their individual ways because of the opportunities the schools provide for personal involvement.

All of these reasons involve comparisons with the public schools. It is probably true that the average public school does have larger classes and places less emphasis on academic development. And it is possible that the average public school is less conducive to moral and personal growth. However, most of the families who send their children to independent schools live in upper middle class neighborhoods. The public schools they could send their children to are usually academically sound. In some cases their laboratories, equipment, and facilities are better than those found in many independent schools. Independent and public schools also use many of the same textbooks, teaching materials, films, and classroom aids. The majority of the students in good public schools plan to go to college and are generally academically oriented. Many good public schools also have special classes for academically superior students as well as a variety of options for students with special interests. One may then ask whether the independent school is, in fact, a better academic setting for learning.

To answer the question as to whether the independent schools are substantially better than the public schools, let us compare the results of our survey for the independent schools and some public schools. Ten public schools were studied at the same time as the independent schools. They were, for the most part, in affluent suburban areas. Students, teachers, and administrators in these schools also completed QUESTA. The students in these schools clearly came from above average homes. The parents in these schools had estimated median annual incomes of approximately $22,000 in 1976. Their incomes exceeded 90 percent of American families in the year of the survey. (To refresh the reader's memory, the median for parents of independent school students was approximately $40,000 in 1976.) Furthermore, their parents were well educated relative to the general population. Some 43 percent of their fathers and 24 percent of their mothers were college graduates (the figures for independent schools were 80 and 60 percent, respectively). These public schools are obviously unusual, but they are probably fairly typical of the public schools which most independent school students would be attending if they went to their local high schools. We thus compared the results for these public school students with those of independent school students.

Academic Programs

The first question many people would ask is whether the schools differ in their academic programs. The survey included questions in several areas which had a bearing on this query. The questions asked about the characteristics of teachers and their teaching practices, the perceived purposes of the schools, and the courses and facilities provided. What were the results? First, these public and independent school teachers did not differ on the number of years they had spent in teaching, the number of years they had worked at their current school, or the highest level of degree they held. Thus, in experience, education, and familiarity with the school, there is little to choose between the public and independent teachers. However, the independent school teacher works with a much smaller number of students in the typical class. The smaller teacher-student ratio allows the independent teacher to do a number of things a public teacher usually cannot do with his or her larger classes. Classroom discussions involving every student, and intensive work with individual students are easier in smaller classes. To some degree, these differences are reflected in students' reports of their teachers' behavior. Compared to the public school students, the students in independent schools more often felt most of their teachers encouraged classroom discussions (74 to 55 percent), and tried to be sure that students understood the work that was done in class (76 to 56 percent). They also more often felt that their teachers were understanding of students' academic problems (47 to 27 percent) and that their teachers were very friendly toward their students outside of class (72 to 31 percent), which might be due to the fact that most of the independent school students were boarding students who had many opportunities to see their teachers during the day. Few students in either type of school believed that their teachers stimulated students to think and be creative, or that teachers succeeded in making their classes interesting to students, but the students in independent schools were somewhat less skeptical on these two counts. Finally, students in independent schools felt fewer of their teachers put emphasis on detailed facts and memorization than did their public counterparts (30 to 47 percent). However, students in the two types of schools did not differ in their descriptions of their teachers' clarity, the relevance of their class materials to current events, the pace at which they presented their material, the extent to which they challenged students, their encouragement of independent work, their encouragement of originality, their involvement of students in choosing class goals, their help to students having difficulty with the work, and their overall success in giving students a broad general understanding of their subject. In sum, students in independent schools seemed to feel closer to their teachers than the students in the public schools in our sample and had more interaction with them. However, in most other aspects of teaching they describe their teachers in about the same terms. The independent school teachers have opportunities for more classroom discussions, and can give students somewhat more individual attention, but in many respects they are like their public school counterparts.

This conclusion is bolstered by the results for the questions on the basis for grading. If there were differences between the ways public and independent school teachers taught their classes, they should be reflected in the behaviors they reward with their grades. For example, if teachers in the elite schools valued creativity or effort, it should be reflected in their grading practices. If teachers emphasized such irrelevant factors as agreement with their views, writing fast on examinations, or a student's family background, they should be reflected in the grades they give. The results showed that students in public and independent schools described their teachers as emphasizing almost exactly the same things. They did not appreciably differ on any of the twelve items about the importance of various factors in getting good grades in their classes. Thus, the independent and public school teachers seemed to look for, and reward the same things in their students' performance.

If the teaching in good public and independent schools is the same in many respects, what about the overall program? A number of questions on the program were asked in our survey. They showed mixed results. For example, although more public school students felt their school offered a good variety of courses (76 percent compared to 56 percent of the independent students), more of the independent school students felt their courses developed students' ability to analyze and criticize written and visual materials (77 to 56 percent). About half the students in both kinds of schools thought the courses offered really useful knowledge or developed really useful skills. In terms of courses offered in creative areas and extracurricular activities available, students in good public schools said, more often than their independent counterparts, that the opportunities were adequate in music and in crafts, such as ceramics and woodworking. Independent school students more often rated the opportunities in photography and films as adequate. There were few differences in students' ratings of the opportunities in theater, painting and graphics, and creative writing. There were no particular differences in the rate of participation in music, painting and graphics, sculpture, and crafts. On balance, it appears that the overall program in these areas is approximately equal, but that independent students tend to participate slightly more. This difference is probably due to the differences in the size of the public and independent schools (Baird, 1969c).

The overall goals of the programs differed. When we asked students to describe the purposes they believed their schools emphasized, independent school students reported more emphasis on preparation for college and intellectual development than the public school students. They more often felt that their schools emphasized helping students get into college (84 to 70 percent), particularly prestigious ones (58 to 32 percent), and preparing their students for the work they would face in college (68 to 42 percent). Independent students also more often felt that their schools emphasized helping students discover and develop their intellectual abilities (62 to 38 percent). Few of the independent students, but still more than the public students, felt their schools emphasized helping students become intellectually independent (32 to 17 percent). Only about a third of the students in either type of school felt their schools emphasized giving students specific knowledge and skills. Thus, although there does not seem to be strong evidence that the teaching and educational opportunities within public and independent schools differed dramatically, the students in independent schools sensed more emphasis on college preparation and intellectual development.

Sense of Community

One advantage often claimed for independent schools is that they are communities, in which students learn to become responsible citizens. The interaction among students, teachers, and administrators is supposed to engender a sense of participation, personal responsibility, and trust. Is there any truth in the claim? One answer to this question is found in the results of the questions we asked about the quality of the communication or understanding between people and groups at the schools. Compared to their counterparts in good public schools, students in the independent schools reported better communication or understanding between student leaders and other students (68 to 51 percent) and groups of students and other groups (60 to 43 percent). However, students in the schools did not differ in their descriptions of the level of understanding between individual students and other individual students, students of one race with another, teachers with individual students, teachers with student groups, teachers with other teachers, administrators with individual students, administrators with student groups, administrators with teachers, counselors with students, and parents with the school. Thus the level of communication or understanding seems to generally be as high in the public schools as in the independent schools, with the possible exceptions of student leaders and groups, a difference that may be due, once again, to the size of the schools.

What about the other aspects of a community, such as the sense of participation and involvement? A series of questions asked students about the influence of various groups on how their school was run. Here, too, students in independent schools felt they had no more influence on their school than did students in good public schools. They also agreed on the relative influence of the head of the school, whether principal or headmaster, other administrators, and so forth. One finding that may not encourage some parents of independent school students is that independent school students felt their parents had no more influence on the schools than did public school students. Students in public and independent schools also did not differ on questions about more specific aspects of involvement in decision-making. Students in both groups of schools felt that they had opportunities to influence change in the school but did not exercise real leadership in areas affecting students. They also felt that students had the freedom to develop their own extracurricular activities. In short, students in the independent sample seemed to feel no more participation in decision making at their schools than did the public sample.

What about the sense of trust? If public school and independent school students' involvement in the activities of their schools did not differ, did they differ in the extent to which they felt they were respected as mature individuals by the adults in the schools? One aspect of trust is revealed when students report what they would do if they had problems. We asked students to whom they would first turn if they needed advice or help in fourteen areas ranging from trouble with classwork to relations with the opposite sex and drugs. The results were virtually identical for students in the independent schools and the good public schools. In most personal areas students would turn to either their friends or their parents. Students in both types of schools would turn to a teacher when they had trouble with classwork, but otherwise they would seldom turn to any of the people in the school for help with any problem. This includes the boarding school housemasters who would be turned to by fewer than 10 percent of the independent school students for any problem. There seems to be no evidence that students feel any greater trust in adults in independent schools than in good public schools.

Influence on Students' Development

Let us now turn to an area in which many independent schools feel proud: the development of students' values and character. Returning to the analyses of the schools' goals, we found that independent school students felt their school emphasized their personal development more than the public school students did. Compared to the public school students, they felt that their schools placed more emphasis on helping students discover and fulfill themselves as persons (70 to 49 percent); helping students be concerned for the needs of others (65 to 44 percent); helping develop students' characters (75 to 60 percent); and preparing students to be good citizens (94 to 72 percent). Students in both types of schools felt their schools emphasized helping students gain an understanding and respect for the rules of society, and molding students according to society's expectations, two purposes that might tend toward conformity. Thus, the students in independent schools seem to give their schools more credit for trying to promote their personal development.

Many independent school headmasters would especially credit their schools with trying to influence a related aspect of students' personal development, the formation of values. School catalogues are filled with references to moral development, ethics, standards of conduct, spiritual values, and the like. In fact, some of the schools were established, not so much to be academically excellent, but to be havens from the moral temptations of the towns. Today, moral temptations are not so easily shut out, but many schools do feel they have a salutory influence on the values of their students. Of course, the independent schools assume that they have much more influence on students' values than do public schools. Is this assumption warranted? There were many questions in our survey which dealt with students' values, as described in Chapter 6. In one question we asked students to choose the three values most personally important to them from a list of thirteen. The choices of the public and independent students were virtually identical, even in the relatively low values they placed on "working hard to achieve academic honors" and "living your religion in your daily life."

In another set of questions we asked students to rate the importance of each of fourteen life goals. Again, the responses of the public and independent school students were virtually the same. Both gave the highest ratings to having a happy family life, finding personal happiness, and understanding other people. Both gave relatively low ratings to engaging in the performance or creation of works of art, becoming leaders in politics, making a contribution to knowledge, and living and working in the world of ideas, among other things. In sum, if the independent schools have a greater influence on the values of their students than do good public schools it is not revealed in students' descriptions of their own values.

Students in both independent and good public schools also seldom credited their schools as sources of their "ethical and spiritual values." In the question about the sources of these values, students in the independent and public schools seldom considered teachers, counselors, school courses in religion, or school courses in other areas as important influences on their values. Only friends, parents, and reading were frequently mentioned. Nearly the same results were obtained when we asked students to rate the importance of various sources on their personal standards concerning sexual behavior: neither public nor independent school adults had much influence, in the view of the students.

What about the subtle values expressed by students when they choose leaders? Again, public and independent school students did not differ in the importance they assigned to fifteen factors in order for a student "to be looked up to by other students" at their schools. The only truly important factors in either type of school were being an open, friendly person and having a pleasing personality. Knowing about literature, art, politics, or making high grades were not very important in either independent or good public schools.

In sum, there seems to be little evidence that independent schools have more impact on the values of their students than good public schools do. Neither type of school seems to have much effect, according to students' reports.

Let us now consider students' overall development. Do public and independent school students differ in their psychological maturity, their social adaptability, or their personal level of functioning? It would take an intense, careful, and lengthy study to begin to answer this question. However, we did ask students to indicate how satisfied they were with their personal development in eighteen areas. The areas ranged from physical growth to the ability to compete without resenting competitors, and from the ability to control emotions to developing a clear sense of oneself. Students in public schools were just as satisfied as students in independent schools in every area.

In a fairly direct assessment of the effects of their schools, students were asked to indicate whether their schools had hindered, had no effect upon, or helped their progress in sixteen areas (see the last chapter for more details). These areas were designed to cover the major developmental tasks of late adolescence, as well as certain academic areas. Public and independent students said their schools had hindered or helped their progress to about the same extent in thirteen of the areas. These included vocational development, relations with parents, self-confidence, independence, ethical or moral sense, responsibility, thinking and reasoning, political awareness, the desire to learn, and aesthetic interests. The three areas in which the independent students felt their schools had helped their progress more often than did the public school students were becoming psychologically independent from their parents, developing the ability to work with people different from themselves, and understanding people who differed from themselves in racial or ethnic background. This is a curious mixture, considering the claims and hopes of the independent schools. The fact that most of the independent schools in our study were boarding schools probably explains the fact that the independent students felt a greater sense of independence from their parents. After all, they *were* independent from their parents in the school. The small size of the schools, combined with the opportunities for interaction with other students would tend to put a premium on good relations with other students.

What have we found in our comparisons of independent and suburban public schools? The independent schools are obviously smaller and many of them are boarding schools. These facts allow teachers and students to have more contact with one another, and also allow smaller classes. The smaller classes allow teachers to give more individual attention to students, to engage in more class discussions, and to have a better understanding of each student's needs. The small size of the schools and the boarding experience may also help students develop their interpersonal skills. However, in most other respects the schools did not differ. Students rated the facilities in good public and independent schools the same. They described many aspects of their teachers' behaviors in the same way although independent school students felt their teachers were more accessible and more concerned with their development. Students in independent schools did not seem to feel they had any better communication with adults in their schools than did the public school students. They felt just as powerless to affect their school. They did not trust the adults in the school to any greater extent than did the public school students. They felt their moral or ethical development was as untouched by the school as did their public counterparts. After several years in the independent schools their values were the same as the students in the public schools. They were just as satisfied with their personal development in many areas, although the independent school students felt they had made more personal progress in several areas.

Some Other Considerations

Despite our results, there may be other reasons, found in information beyond our study, which would strengthen the case for a family's decision to choose an independent school. For example, the teachers in independent schools are often more knowledgeable about their subject matter than teachers in public schools. From Kraushaar's reports on their educational preparation, they have liberal arts or science educations with major field specialties rather than school of education specialties. Their motivations for working in independent schools seem primarily academic; they wish to be able to teach their subject in their own ways. This, coupled with the lower salaries they obtain, suggests that they are committed to educating students. They seem to make their choices as they have because of love for their subject, for teaching, or for both. There are many good teachers in the public schools, of course, but it would probably be fair to say that a student's chances of encountering many good teachers are higher in the elite independent schools than in most public schools. The chance that students can find a teacher who will encourage their interests and intense investigations of special topics is considerably greater in the independent schools, because of the backgrounds of the teachers and the fact that they are available in the evenings and on weekends. Furthermore, since the average independent school class is only half the size of the average public high school class, the student is considerably more likely to have helpful interaction with his or her teachers in the independent school.

Another plus for the independent school is the character of the students. The majority are bright, academically oriented, and believe in the worth of a college education. Thus, a student who goes to a selective independent school will interact predominantly with students who value education and intellectual attainment. Research has shown that the composition of the student body at a school can sometimes have resounding effects on the value students place on academic work and further education. Bright, academically oriented students sometimes put forth less effort or plan to go to college less often when they attend schools with few students like themselves than when they attend schools with many students like themselves. As suggested in the chapter on the effects of the schools, the independent schools may be extremely effective by simply keeping students at the same high level of academic motivation and intellectual curiosity they had when they entered the schools. Yet another consideration is that, with the possible exception of their college years, the independent school students will probably never be surrounded by so many bright and lively people again in their lives. Perhaps it is this aspect of the experience that keeps some independent school graduates talking about their school days the rest of their lives.

The intellectual capacity of the students also allows the school to provide an intensely stimulating environment. When students are at about the same high level of academic ability, teachers can use techniques designed for a narrow range of ability, thereby making their teaching more effective. In most public schools, teachers have to use somewhat different approaches with students with different talents, thereby diluting their overall effectiveness for any particular group of students. In the independent schools, teachers can concentrate their efforts on the one teaching strategy they feel will work best with their students for any particular topic, thereby increasing their potential impact on students' learning.

Another consequence of the intellectual ability of the students is that it allows the schools to emphasize academic rigor and challenge. As emphasized throughout this book, independent schools do emphasize high academic standards of learning and performance, an emphasis seldom matched in most public schools. These standards challenge the students' abilities and self-discipline. Although "challenge" may seem an old fashioned and even musty idea to some educators, there are good reasons to believe that many students learn more when they must stretch themselves to meet high expectations. The schools also have the advantage of being able to *reward* high levels of academic performance. Students reinforce each others' academic bent by their informal discussions, mutual concern, and just by the fact that they are all academically able. The small classes, and the values of the schools also encourage the teachers to reward academic performance.

The small enrollments of the schools, combined with the variety of their curricular and extracurricular programs also allow the schools to provide unusual opportunities for their students. There is convincing evidence that small schools encourage participation by their students. The clearest example is a play—for example, Ibsen's *An Enemy of the People*, which involves eleven main characters and at least half a dozen "extras," plus people to construct the sets, stage hands, people to work the lights, collect the tickets, make the advertisements, etc. In addition, stand-ins for the main characters need to be ready to step in if anything happens. A minimum of forty to fifty students would be needed to produce this play—one that involves fewer characters than many others. Thus, in a school with 400 students, about one in ten students would be *directly* involved in the play, and many more would be involved vicariously. If the play were limited to a single class, such as twelfth graders, nearly half the students in that grade might be directly involved with the play. In contrast, if the same play were put on in a school with 2,000 students, about one in fifty students would be involved, or, if presented by a class, one in twelve. As this example suggests, school activities in small schools require the involvement of a high percentage of the students. Since the schools have many activities, programs, and events, most students are involved in some activity most of the time. This means that students in independent schools, which are typically fairly small, experience an unusually wide variety of activities, enabling them to exercise many talents and roles. Consequently, students can develop a wide range of interests, and have opportunities to discover their own talents and interests in particular fields. The wide range of sports offered at most schools—from LaCrosse to cross-country skiing, from tennis to diving, from rock climbing to kayaking—along with the emphasis on intramural and interscholastic sports, means that students of all ages, skills, and interests have the opportunity to be actively involved in sports. Furthermore, the range of sports offered to the students makes it likely that students can find a sport they can pursue throughout their lives—a much healthier approach to sports than the pattern in some public schools, where the few students on varsity teams are active, while the rest are primarily spectators. Likewise, the wide variety of stimulating experiences available—from years in France to mini-courses on the idea of the Imperial presidency—mean that students can experience and discover ideas and interests they may make their life work, or simply enjoy the rest of their lives.

Finally, nearly all of the schools emphasize the moral development of their students as one of their important functions, and some of them provide religious instruction or observation. For families who feel that their children would profit from moral or religious instruction, combined with high level academic instruction, the schools provide a very attractive option. Families who feel that values and religion are important should be able to choose schools which emphasize training in those areas, and some of the independent schools may be their best alternative. The pluralism of American education and society virtually require the existence of such options.

Having said all this, we should remember that the intensity of the elite school experience can be as disturbing as it can be conducive to growth. As one school put it in its description of itself, "The aspect of [this school] , which gives the school its usefulness and meaning, is challenge. When a boy comes to [this school] he is stripped of any self-righteousness; he learns what will be expected of him by the school, his peers, and himself. He is confronted with a great choice in values; whether to master the school or be mastered by it. For those who accept the challenge, who strive to meet the demands and overcome the many obstacles of school life, the school has a magnetism, reflected in the person's attitudes; but for those who decide otherwise, the school loses its true meaning and becomes an institution to be endured" *Secondary School Admission Test* (1971). The comments of the students throughout the preceding chapters suggest that many students feel they must endure many things in their schools. Again, whether the student and the school will be happy with one another depends on the student's maturity and interests, the school's program and adaptability, and the fit between them.

Conclusions

It is hard to give a clear answer to our original question as to whether a family should spend between $10,000 and $20,000 to send a child to independent school. We have seen that in many respects independent schools are very similar to good public schools, although they do have smaller classes which allow teachers to give individual attention to students and lead students to feel they have made greater personal progress in several areas. Given these facts, it would appear that the decision is a matter depending on individual students and individual schools. If parents feel that their children would profit from greater individual attention than they would get in their public schools in order to reach their potential, then the independent school may be the best alternative. If the children work as well in moderate to large classes as small classes, then parents would need to have some other compelling reason to send their child to independent school. Likewise, if parents are convinced that their local public high school would be a poor place to send their children, then they should consider independent schools. It all depends on how well a particular school fits the needs of a particular student and how well a particular student fits the emphases of a particular school. The better the fit, the more confidently we can say "Yes, a family should seriously consider this independent school for their child." The choice must be based on a realistic assessment of a student's needs and an objective consideration of the emphases of the schools. (The family considering an independent school should read John Esty's book *Choosing a Private School*, a realistic guide to examining the strong and weak points of schools, as well as a useful source of suggestions for making a wise decision.) If the choice is made wisely, it is likely the student will have a satisfying secondary education. Perhaps the strongest recommendation for an independent school education is that it at least makes a *choice* possible.

9 The Challenge of the Future

This chapter deals with the future of the elite schools from three perspectives. The first perspective is based on reports of some changes in the schools which occurred in the last few years since the original survey of the schools. The second perspective comes from an examination of the directions in which the people in the schools believe the schools should move in the future. The problems of effecting change are also discussed. The final perspective is a discussion of the future role of the schools in American education and society.

Change and Stability: The Schools in the Mid-70s

The late 60s and early 70s were a period of powerful changes in society and education. Students of that period were stunned by the shootings of Martin Luther King and Robert Kennedy. They saw the demonstrations at Columbia and San Francisco State, and other colleges on television. Later the same medium allowed them to participate both in the crowning achievement of technology, the first landing of men on the moon, and in an international tragedy, the war in Biafra. In the next year, their examinations were disturbed by the Cambodian invasion and shootings at Kent State and Jackson State.

The events in society were paralleled by ferment and dissent in the elite schools. Although much of the activity of students was directed toward national and international problems, much was also directed toward the schools themselves, a reaction which might be expected. In a period of rapid change, traditional patterns appeared irrelevant to the critical issues of concern to the students. Likewise, the schools' heavy emphasis on academic learning may have, in the view of the students, seem misguided and far from their concern for human sympathy and ways to change society. Even when the content of courses bears on social issues, it usually neglects discussions of ways to translate classroom knowledge into community and social action.

The students' questioning attitudes led, in many schools, to student unrest. Alan Blackmer (1970) has described the targets of this unrest: lack of student influence in shaping school rules and policy; poor communication between students and faculty, students not listened to; school life too tightly scheduled and regimented; too little time for oneself; overly strict regulations of dress codes and hair styles; too much pressure for grades; and boredom. These topics were widely discussed and debated within the schools during the early 1970s.

135

What was the result? Were there changes in the schools? Or did the swing in students' thinking back to compliance and privatism in the mid-1970s, as noted by Yankelovich (1974), leave the schools pretty much as they were?

To answer these questions, a resurvey of many of the schools with the questionnaires was undertaken three years later, when any changes or their lack should have been apparent. The results are sobering for those who expect great changes. First, the students who came to the schools were the same type of bright, academically-oriented students with well educated, financially comfortable parents who have high ambitions for their children. The students cited the same, mainly academic, reasons for choosing their schools, and they had the same hopes and apprehensions about their schools. They hoped to go to college, particularly the "better" ones. They still anticipated rigorous academic demands and few personal problems.

The results for the teachers showed them to have about the same backgrounds, educations, and views of their roles and responsibilities. All of these results indicate that the people in the schools in the mid 70s are the same kind of people as those in the late 60s and early 70s, which would suggest that the possibilities for change are limited. The physical settings of the schools are the same, including, for many schools, their isolation, and their rural atmospheres. The basic curriculum, oriented toward college preparation has also changed only slightly. There may be more electives today, but the basic emphasis on English, mathematics, science, and languages remains unchanged. In short, if the same kind of students are taught the same courses by the same teachers, in the same classrooms, buildings and grounds, how much change is possible?

The results on students' personal goals suggest that there was, in fact, little change. Students were still concerned with personal happiness, a happy family life, friendship, being independent, and standing up for their own rights. Although students were as uninterested in political office as ever, there was some decline in the percentage who hoped to "change the world for the better." (This result introduces a theme which will appear in other results.) Students said their values had come from the same sources as in the early 70s, and, although there has been some improvement in communication in the schools, teachers and administrators had the same misconceptions of students' sources of values.

Students also held approximately the same views on a wide variety of issues. They still thought relationships between the ethnic and racial groups at their schools were friendly and based on the individual's characteristics, not the groups. They still thought that the teaching was individualized, thorough, demanding, and generally good. They still felt the same way about the basis for awarding grades. Their perceptions of the importance of talking a lot in discussions and being friendly with the teacher still disagreed with the views of the teachers. And so on it goes, with the same patterns of results in counseling, extracurricular activities, etc.

But what about the areas Blackmer identified as the foci of unrest? Has anything changed there after all the controversy and dissent? To answer that question for the first of Blackmer's areas, the lack of student influence on school policy, we can turn to the results on students' views of power in the school. Students in the mid-70s did seem to feel that their school head had slightly less power than did students in the early 70s, although the school head was still seen as the most powerful person in the school. However, they reported no increase in the *students'* influence on the school. They felt they lack power and play, at best, a minor role in the way the school is run. The results of the questions on the quality of communication, bearing on Blackmer's second area, lack of communication, suggest some progress. Students seem somewhat more positive about their communication with the administration. Although only a slight majority think the communication is good, there still has been improvement. Perhaps this improvement is due to the various arrangements for better communication set up in many schools after the earlier unrest of the late 60s and early 70s. Committees, open-house hours, regular meetings, and open discussion sessions have become common at many schools.

Students' dissatisfaction with their schools' regimentation and the lack of time to themselves (Blackmer's third area) has not decreased. They still feel they need more privacy, more free time and more things to do, of their own choosing, when they do have free time. This is related to one of Blackmer's later areas: boredom. Perhaps it would be difficult to open up the schedule if the schools are to adhere to their rigorous academic demands. However, since the students are bright and highly motivated, it should be possible to allow a good deal more self-study and independent work, which could be done according to the students' schedules. Self-study does not necessarily entail any lowering of standards, and it could relieve some of the pressures of regimentation.

The rules and regulations which irritated so many students in the first survey have been changed in many schools. Uniforms, jackets and ties, and the like are seen at few schools. Instead, students demonstrate the usual adolescent conformity to their peer group's tastes in clothing, hair style, and grooming. Students were much more satisfied with rules about dress and hair styles in the second survey. They were also much more satisfied with rules in a number of areas reflecting their freedom of action. The areas showing the most change were: smoking, control of student publications, freedom to leave school during free periods, permission to leave school for the day, required attendance at classes and assemblies, and freedom to organize meetings. Overall, these results suggest a general relaxation of rules and regulations to allow students considerably more latitude in their behavior out of class. The extent of relaxation should not be exaggerated, however. The schools are still constrained by legal liability for their students, and consequently need to know where they are, and need to have reasonable assurances that they are not in physical or psychological danger.

The results of the questions on stresses on students bear on Blackmer's remaining area, pressures for grades. Students felt they experienced just as much stress from pressures for grades in the second survey as they did in the first. The academic emphases of the schools and the academic plans of the students leave little room for lessening scholastic demands. Interestingly, perhaps because of the decline in radical activity in the 1970s, students much less often said they were bothered by national and international problems and by relations among racial and ethnic groups in the second survey. One consequence of the decline in concern about political issues is that pressures for grades are the most stressful aspect of adolescence for most students in the elite schools. Grades were a greater source of stress than worries about getting into college, relations with the opposite sex, pressures from parents, or deciding about religious beliefs. Thus, although students' concerns about grades have not appreciably increased, other concerns have become less important, so grades have become the most critical problem in the lives of many students. Of course, "pressures for grades" can mean many things, including personal ambition to do well, the need to get good grades for college, parental expectations, the academic requirements of the school, and the performance demanded by teachers. As diverse as these appear, they all revolve around the central academic purposes of the schools.

This last point is related to other results, which clearly show that academic purposes still dominate the schools. The three purposes which students and adults think are most strongly emphasized in the schools are still: first, to help students get into college; second, to prepare students for the work they will face in college; and third, to help students discover and develop their intellectual abilities. The general pattern for the purposes people in the schools believed were emphasized was generally the same as the pattern analyzed in Chapter 6. There were some shifts from the first survey to the second, however. People felt that there is more emphasis on helping students become concerned for the needs of others and on helping students become independent thinkers. They felt there was less emphasis on getting into prestigious colleges, perhaps reflecting the lower probability that independent school graduates will get into the very best colleges simply by virtue of their elite school backgrounds.

The general pattern of purposes people felt should be emphasized also remained the same, with the exceptions that more students felt that emphasis should be placed on helping students understand and respect the rules of society, and more felt emphasis should be placed on preparing students for jobs.

Overall, then, the schools do not appear to have changed in any fundamental sense during the last few years. The chief change seems to be a relaxation or elimination of petty and annoying rules. Students seem to feel less irritation from a number of small aspects of their schools, which has probably lessened the overall level of tension. However, the central academic purposes of the schools are emphasized as strongly as ever, and the pressures, organization, and intensity of the environment which are the consequences of these purposes remain. Some possible ways to restructure the environments of the schools will be discussed in the following pages.

Need for Further Change

We have just seen that the schools have changed in some ways. In what areas do the people in the schools desire further change? To answer this question, a block of items was included in the study that dealt directly with the issue of needed change. Sixteen areas were included. The areas where students seemed to want change the most, whether or not there have been earlier attempts were: the curriculum, rules and regulations, student government, off-campus programs, and teacher-student relations. Teachers saw particular need for new or continued change in the curriculum, rules and regulations, teaching techniques, drug education, and student government. All of these are *relative* emphases, however, since the majority of every group recommended either new or continued change in virtually every area. The only areas where any groups were *relatively* satisfied were the yearly schedule, and athletics or physical education. Students, teachers, and administrators in every kind of school sought continued or new change in nearly every area.

These results are supported and amplified by the results reported in earlier chapters. For example, we saw that students would prefer less emphasis on academic knowledge in courses, and more emphasis on the students' personal development. The details of dissatisfaction with the rules and regulations were discussed in Chapter 5. The desire for better communication in the schools was also described earlier.

Given these desires for changes, how can they be accomplished? In the public sector there has been a good deal of talk about developing "change agents" in the schools. There is also a lot of general rhetoric about reforming the schools. The reformers seem to assume that, with the right technique, changes can be made smoothly and quickly. And, once the change is made, the reformers feel that the conditions which prompted the change will automatically also be changed. However, as Sarason (1971) has pointed out, one can change the content of a curriculum, change activities, and change how people talk and change what people say about the schools, but everyday life in the classroom and in the school may remain the same. To change complicated organizations requires a different way of thinking than the way we think of changing individuals.

Perhaps more basic than such tactical problems as trying to change everything at once, are the false analogies to the school. One of the favorite analogies—industrial organizations—often leads educators to uncritically adopt such industrial techniques as sensitivity training which are ill-suited for the schools, as Sarason (1971) has pointed out. These techniques leave the impression that "interpersonal relations" are the most important cause of problems in the schools, when such things as traditional expectations held for teachers and students, routines, and irrelevant requirements are usually much more important.

How then, can one begin to change the schools? The first is to talk to the people in the schools—the concerned students, teachers, and administrators—about what they think is the place to begin. Discussions among these groups are often helpful. These discussions may reveal that the groups know little about each other, as we suggested in the chapter on communication. For example, the groups (and the person or group forcing change) may have very unrealistic time perspectives, partly because they may not view time perspectives as a problem. The administrators may think of changes in terms of four-year cycles, the teachers may be thinking of changes to be accomplished in a year or two, and students may feel changes must be made within the week to be relevant. Students may be unrealistically impatient, but administrators may feel insufficient urgency in carrying out changes.

Even when they are implemented, many changes rapidly lose their innovative quality. Often, the reason is that the changes have been imposed from the top down without taking into account the feelings and opinions of those who will have to implement the changes. This is not to say that the cooperation of the school head is not necessary for almost all changes, but to indicate that single-handed, arbitrary changes will usually have little effect. Changes are also often short-lived when they are based on a single view of the situation. A school that recognizes a problem needs to consider a wide variety of alternatives before beginning changes. Yet another reason that changes fail is that programs can become ends in themselves, rather than activities that are designed to alter conditions that had created a problem at the school.

One of the most important reasons that changes often fail is that people promoting change do not consider the realities of school life because of their one-sided views of the school. This is partly due to the invisibility of the culture of the school. One cannot see this culture in the same way one can see the individuals in the school; consequently, many reformers often know far less about the actual functioning of the school than they usually assume, and this assumption leads to their errors. This may happen especially frequently when the reformers are outside "experts." "Experts" usually come from a completely different social culture, such as the university, and their understanding of the school's culture and the ways it may be changed are limited. They may assign little value to the traditions of the schools which define its character.

With all these drawbacks, how can the schools change themselves? Perhaps the most fundamental step is to realize that there may be several "schools," depending on the group and the person. The next step is to realize that changes in titles and forms mean little. The effective changes are those that change the habitual actions of the people in the schools, what Sarason has called the behavioral regularities. It is not enough to have a sensitivity training conference, if the next day students and teachers meet each other in the same situations, with the same roles, and do the same things. Fundamentally, we need to change our ways of thinking about changes.

Many changes have been superficial or ephemeral for the reasons suggested above. However, many changes have been important and permanent. These changes have usually reflected some critical need of the school. The directions of the changes have usually been to create more humane, informal, relaxed and comfortable environments, while retaining the academic rigor of the schools. The course of change has not always been smooth, but the changes do not seem to have changed the basic goals of the schools.

The Future of the Elite Schools

The future of the elite schools is tied to the future of our society financially and philosophically. The problems of financing and budgeting may mean that some schools may need state or federal aid to maintain their quality or even to survive. The people in the schools now seem opposed to state aid, according to Kraushaar's results, but they seem to be cautiously considering the possibility. Another possibility is that some educational voucher system will be adopted at the state or federal level. Other changes in tax laws or programs could make a large difference in the budgets of the schools. (The reader is referred to Kraushaar's excellent discussions of these issues.) All of these trends could strongly affect the schools. In lieu of such changes, the current financial squeeze may have a powerful influence on some schools. Some of the schools, facing extinction, may try to survive by becoming less selective in their admission of students, or they may abandon their traditional curricula to encompass whatever subjects are currently popular, or they may try to appeal to a single kind of clientele. These ways of dealing with financial pressures may be damaging to the schools. On the other hand, to other schools financial pressures may act as a healthy stimulus to rethink their purposes.

The chief purpose of most of the elite schools has been a rather single-minded pursuit of traditional academic excellence. As the earlier chapters indicate, this emphasis on the academic had led the schools to develop effective and all-encompassing environments for learning literature, mathematics, languages, science, and history. The schools are extremely good places to learn these things. The visitor to elite school campuses cannot fail to be impressed with the scholarly atmosphere exemplified by the schools' libraries, buildings, and laboratories. Talking to the students, the visitor will be impressed by their knowledge and articulateness. The teachers he or she meets will usually be committed to their subject and their school. Many of the textbooks for the eleventh and twelfth grades are designed for freshmen or sophomores in college. The authors of the books students carry around to read for their own pleasure include Camus, Hesse, Jung, and Tolstoy. It is clear that the schools' atmospheres are permeated with an emphasis on scholastic achievement, and that the schools encourage students to value academic success. The records of the numbers of students who continue their educations in selective colleges and selective graduate and professional schools is ample proof of the success of the schools in their academic purpose. As a result of this purpose, many of the most prominent and successful individuals in America were educated in the elite schools. However, as we have shown in this book, there is another side to the press for academic excellence. Success has its price. Many of the students in our sample felt pressure from the demands of the school, many were convinced of the irrelevance of their studies, and many complained about the lack of provisions for individual expression and growth.

Traditional schools were designed to prepare students for a niche in a society of conventional values. The need today is to make the school fit the needs of students ready to enter an unconventional—and unpredictable—society rather than to fit the student to the school. To accomplish this change, the schools could consider a variety of alternatives to traditional patterns. For example, Kraushaar suggests changing the role of the teacher from the authoritarian lecturer to the manager of a central learning center filled with audiovisual equipment, kits, equipment, programmed teaching machines, books, and records, all of which would be designed for student use. The student could use these materials according to a flexible schedule managed by the teacher. There would be less emphasis on particular subject areas, and greater stress on the interconnections of knowledge in different fields. There would also be more emphasis on values, attitudes and feelings in the proposed school than in the old. There would also be more emphasis on the arts. Another possible reform is the involvement of students in school decision making. The idea is to have students experience democracy directly rather than as a theoretical proposition which was denied by their daily experiences.

All of these changes can be approached piecemeal, but a single change in one part of a school's environment is often submerged by the weight of tradition in the rest of the school. Changes in specific areas need to be related to changes in the overall atmosphere of the school, making the school a place to foster independence rather than dependence, a center of contact with the real world rather than a protected hothouse, and an arena for responsibility rather than irrelevance.

Many schools have begun all sorts of experiments in the areas just described as well as many others. The experiments have had mixed success, but at a minimum, they show that changes will not damage the schools. The experiments, including independent study programs, broader course offerings, community internship programs, and various schemes for involving students in decision-making at the schools, have often had the positive effects expected for them. Students involved in the changes seem to feel that the schools are in better contact with the real world. Relaxation of dress codes, rules, and regulations may be making the schools more comfortable places for the students. But are these changes sufficient to meet the criticisms voiced by the students and teachers in this study? The basic strength and the basic weakness of the schools seem to remain the same: the great emphasis on traditional academic excellence. A number of the schools have tried to change their "pressure cooker" academic atmospheres by offering more courses and allowing more credit for such "nonacademic" activities as art, music, dance, independent science experiments, drama, and involvement in the community. These efforts seem to have relieved the pressures to some degree, but, in most schools, the emphasis is still on high level academic achievement. Of course, although the schools do this job rather well, they are not completely successful. As Gaines (1972) puts it:

Academic excellence is the simplest and surely the most honest objective of the prestige schools. And in general they do provide a strong foundation in a selected set of disciplines. Their students do amass a considerable amount of factual knowledge; do learn something about problem-solving, analytical thinking, and techniques of research; do gain a certain control of their own language and an ability to express themselves; do develop relatively high standards of performance; do on occasion even evolve a modicum of intellectual curiosity. But for what purpose? Is any effort made to arouse a passion for truth or understanding? Is knowledge presented in a context of joy and wonder and excitement? Is that why all the way through school kids are constantly being classified by means of test scores, grades, rank in class, etc.? Personally, I no longer take very seriously our prestige schools' commitment to academic excellence (that is, as contributing to a richer freer life, rather than merely as a step toward 'making it' in the affluent society).

If the schools are to change, in which direction should they move and how should they do it? In my opinion, they would have difficulty moving away from their role of providing first-class academic educations. The schools have performed this function for many years, and they would violate their traditions and blur their identity were they to abandon it. Furthermore, it is this overall emphasis that truly distinguishes the schools from other schools. In contrast to Gaines, I do take the schools' commitment to academic excellence seriously, but, in agreement with him, I think that they have focused on an excessively narrow interpretation of intellectual tasks. In their search for excellence, many schools have raised the level of academic performance, believing that this practice would increase the quality and level of achievement of their students. This trend has led to a situation which has been described as the "academic pressure cooker." Many educators feel that these practices will result in students with greater capacity, not only for grades, but for achievements in such important areas of human endeavor as leadership, science, writing, and the expressive arts. They believe that students who have high academic aptitude and are required to achieve at high levels academically, will be much more likely than other students to achieve at high levels in other areas.

Recent research has cast doubt on that belief by examining the relation between academic intelligence and creative behavior and high level accomplishment (Nichols and Holland, 1963; Holland and Richards, 1965; Hoyt, 1966;

Richards et al., 1967; Baird, 1976). All of these studies have indicated that academic ability and achievement are not strongly related to achievement in other areas. A few authors, e.g., Nichols and Holland (1964), have conducted artificial "selection" studies and have found that if students were selected on the basis of academic aptitude or performance, the rate of creative achievements in college would be considerably less than if students were selected on the basis of high school nonacademic achievements. (These creative and social achievements refer to high-level accomplishments which presumably require originality, complex skills, long-term persistence, and generally receive public recognition.) A review by Hoyt (1966) of forty-six studies concerning the relation of college grades to adult success has indicated that academic achievement also does not have a high correlation with later success in life. Thus, we conclude that there is no evidence for a strong relation between academic, social and creative accomplishment.

However, many of the same studies just cited indicate that nonacademic or creative achievement at one stage predicts later success in the same areas of achievement. (Also see the reviews by Taylor and Holland, 1964; and Baird, 1976). Furthermore, studies of eminent persons (e.g., Cox, 1926) have shown that achievement begins early. Eiduson (1962) found that the research scientists in her sample (including some Nobel prize winners) had frequently begun creative work in high school and college. Studies of eminent persons in other groups (e.g., Matthew's 1960 study of United States senators) indicate that people who are later eminent begin activity in their area early.

How might school teachers and administrators make use of these findings? First, they could realize that education based solely on academic criteria offers no guarantee that their schools will produce students who are likely to achieve outside the classroom. If they are interested *only* in classroom achievement, their present procedures are appropriate. But if they are interested in other kinds of achievement, they must look for many kinds of talent in their students and attempt to develop these talents in the students who have them. By focusing on these other kinds of talent, the schools can educate students who will be more likely to achieve in such areas as science, art, leadership, music, writing, and drama.

How might the schools change to encompass a wider view of excellence? First, they could broaden the possible curricular experiences. This breadth should, however, not preclude an intense approach in a narrow area for the students who are intensely interested in special subjects. For example, a student should be able to read, discuss, and research a wide field of subject matter or work intensely on a specific problem, whether it is the common themes in Hesse's novels or a difficult problem in mathematical theory. The curriculum should therefore be flexible, allowing the student to take unusual combinations of courses, special classes, or to get credit for reading in special areas. However, the students should not be allowed to proceed helter-skelter through the courses.

The student needs good counsel and advice in the construction of a curricular plan. The counseling should be based on a careful assessment of the student's needs, interests, and talents.

Teachers could change their behavior from that of trying to get the students to master as much material as possible in nine months to other kinds of behavior which may stimulate more real learning among the students. One way would be for the teachers to share their own scholarly and research interests, demonstrating how they approach a topic or problem, how they gather information, how they make a start, how they cope with failures, how they reach conclusions, and how they produce their end product whether it is a poem, an experiment, a mathematical proof, or a scientific article. In other words, students can see how real productive work is done, and, consequently, should be better able to do similar work of their own. Another possibility is for teachers to involve some of their students in their own research or scholarly work.

Another area of change is extracurricular activities. The line between extracurricular and curricular activities could be eliminated, as it is in real life. Many schools could well afford to lessen the time required for classwork, and increase the time for extracurricular activities. The areas outside the classroom could also be greatly expanded to be major parts of the school. Perhaps some schools could specialize in art, some in writing, some in science, and some in other areas. (Wykham Rise is an example of a school concentrating on the fine and performing arts.) These measures could help the elite schools become schools for excellence in many areas, and, in the process, they should become more exciting places to learn and teach.

What about the need expressed by so many students and radical critics, to make the schools more humane and relaxed? Many of the schools have stressed acceptance of authority, respect for the traditional, and conformity to conventional standards. Some reformers want to turn the schools into communities based on love, warmth, and cooperation rather than competition. These are very worthy goals, but there is little reason to believe that radical reforms will necessarily create these virtues any more successfully than the traditional schools created the virtues they sought. The schools are limited in what they can do, and the power of innovations to revamp the school have probably been exaggerated. Furthermore, excellence and comfort are not always completely compatible. Certainly, excellence demands hard work and the teacher who draws the best performance from his or her students often needs to be demanding. My point is simply that, to remain centers of excellence, the schools may not be able to be as relaxed or warm as reformers demand, at least in the *way* some reformers demand. However, the schools can change many things which are unrelated to the pursuit of a variety of forms of excellence. We have seen many examples in earlier chapters. They include the further elimination of petty rules, decreasing formality, increasing the quality of communication in the school, and deemphasizing pressures for strictly academic excellence. These changes seem feasible and, in some cases, necessary, to improve the quality of life for everyone in the schools.

The elite independent schools are a part of America. They have served their function of providing the highest quality of academic education for many years. They still have a critical role to play in the United States, as places where educational experiments can be tried, where those who do not choose the public schools can send their children, where specific traditions can be followed, and where there are some guarantees that quality in education will be maintained. If America is to remain a pluralistic society, it must have pluralism in its schools. The elite schools help maintain that pluralism and the choice of actions and values which it fosters. If the elite schools could also vary the kinds of excellence they train, they could substantially increase the pluralism of educational choices in America and would consequently increase the variety of human excellence that makes for a great civilization.

Appendix A:
Basic Data

The data for this book came from a project to develop an instrument which could assess the way people in schools perceive the environment of the school—the interplay among its people, processes, and things. Important dimensions of the environment include the way each individual feels about himself and the perceptions, values, expectations, satisfactions, and dissatisfactions of the various groups that make up a school community. To enable secondary schools to generate this kind of information about their individual environments, the Secondary School Research Program (SSRP) developed QUESTA.

Although QUESTA I and QUESTA II were developed separately, the process was the same for both. A Working Committee of teachers and administrators from member schools of the SSRP prepared an analysis of the areas of information they judged would be most useful for secondary schools. This analysis of information was used as a basis for examining related educational, psychological, and sociological research which revealed several operational approaches that the committee members reviewed and discussed with staff members of Educational Testing Service (ETS).

The next step was to develop a preliminary version of an instrument consisting of questions based on the work done so far and on suggestions from previous research. The preliminary version was reviewed and revised by students, teachers, administrators, and counselors at SSRP schools as well as by staff members of ETS, including program directors from the Institutional Research Program for Higher Education, the Secondary School Admission Test, the National Teacher Examinations, and research psychologists from the Developmental Research Division. This revision was followed by further interviews with students to determine their reactions to the questions. A second version of the instrument was developed from the results of these reviews and interviews. It was then reviewed and revised by the Working Committee. The final task of shaping the questionnaire for the trial administrations was carried out by ETS staff members.

The instrument was administered to students, teachers, and administrators in independent schools, ten public schools, and four Catholic schools. The independent schools were located in the northeast (twenty-nine), the mid-Atlantic states (six), the Midwest (two), the South (three), and the Far West (two). Nineteen were in rural settings, thirteen in small towns, and ten in suburban or urban areas. Five had formal ties to a church group, although a number of others have some commitment to Christianity or religion in general. Eleven had senior class sizes of twenty-five to fifty, fourteen class sizes of fifty to one hundred, and seventeen class sizes of more than one hundred. The majority (twenty-three) were boys' schools, nine were girls' schools, five were coeducational schools, and five were coordinate schools. Seven were day schools; the rest were predominantly boarding schools, although most of these had some day students. Although all were expensive, and consequently the parents were fairly well to do, the schools varied in the relative affluence of the parents. In the judgments of two experts who were very knowledgeable about independent schools, twelve of the schools drew students from slightly affluent homes, sixteen drew students from moderately affluent homes, and fourteen drew students from very affluent homes. Similarly, although all the schools had fairly selective admissions, some were more selective than others. The same two experts also judged the selectivity of the schools; they judged thirteen of the schools to be somewhat selective, seventeen to be moderately selective, and twelve to be highly selective. The same judges used a five-point scale to rate the intensity of the schools' emphasis on academic achievement. On this scale 1 represented a low academic emphasis, five a very high academic emphasis. The judges thought seven schools deserved a 1 rating, three a 2 rating, ten a 3 rating, seventeen a 4 rating, and five a 5 rating. Many of the schools have been included in various lists of "eminent schools," "gentlemen's schools," and prestigious schools for girls. Thus, the schools in the sample represented a diverse and typical cross-section of prestigious independent schools.

The ten public schools were generally located in affluent suburbs of major cities. Geographically, four were located in the midwest, three in the northeast, two in mid-Atlantic states, and one in the southwest. The four Catholic schools came from the South, the Midwest, and the mid-Atlantic states.

QUESTA

QUESTA II, the Questionnaire for Students, Teachers and Administrators was administered to eleventh and twelvth graders in all these schools in the spring of 1970 and to many of them again in the spring of 1974. From this instrument a school gains information about the degree to which students, faculty members, and administrators are satisfied with various parts of the school and with student development, about the nature and values of the school's subgroups, and about sources of tension and dissatisfaction. By comparing certain sections of both instruments, the school can measure its impact upon the student's attitudes and values. QUESTA is designed to assess the school, not individuals, so it is completed without any identification of individuals, and the results are tabulated and reported for groups only. In addition, a parallel instrument, the Questionnaire for New Students, was administered to new entering students in most of the same schools in the fall of 1971. The composition of the sample of schools was almost the same; the schools from the QUESTA sample which did not administer the Questionnaire for New Students were replaced by schools which were very similar.

The Questionnaire for New Students (QUESTA I) is administered at the beginning of high school. This instrument gathers attitudinal, biographical, demographic, and socioeconomic information and is designed to discover a student's attitudes toward himself, his peers, his previous school, and his new school—his hopes, fears, and aspirations.

Two forms of QUESTA were administered; 1,702 independent school students, 298 teachers, and 142 administrators completed Form A; 1,695 students, 297 teachers, and 148 administrators completed Form B. All respondents were encouraged to write their reactions to their schools, the questionnaire or any other topic they wished to say something about on a separate "Comments Sheet." These comments were subject to a content analysis, and aided our interpretation of the data.

Some 4,600 entering students completed the Questionnaire for New Students shortly before they entered their schools or within a week or two after entry.

Both QUESTA I and QUESTA II have subsequently been revised to be useful in all types of schools. Further information about them may be obtained from Educational Testing Service.

Appendix B:
Schools in QUESTA Samples

Boarding Schools

Name	Location
Abbot Academy	Andover, Mass.
Belmont Hill School	West Concord, Mass.
Cheshire School	Cheshire, Conn.
Cushing Academy	Ashburnham, Mass.
Dana Hall School	Wellesley, Mass.
Deerfield Academy	Deerfield, Mass.
Governer Dummer Academy	Byfield, Mass.
Groton School	Groton, Mass.
Hebron Academy	Hebron, Maine
The Hill School	Pottstown, Pa.
The Hotchkiss School	Lakeville, Conn.
Kent School	Kent, Conn.
The Lawrence Academy	Groton, Mass.
The Lawrenceville School	Lawrenceville, N.J.
Loomis School[a]	Windsor, Conn.
Mary C. Wheeler School	Providence, R.I.
The Masters School (Dobbs)	Dobbs Ferry, N.Y.
Milton Academy	Milton, Mass.
Mt. Hermon School[b]	Mt. Hermon, Mass.
The Peddie School	Hightstown, N.J.
Phillips Academy	Andover, Mass.
Pomfret School	Pomfret, Conn.
Miss Porter's School	Farmington, Conn.
St. Mark's School	Southborough, Mass.
St. Paul's School	Concord, N.H.
Salisbury School	Salisbury, Conn.
Tabor Academy	Marion, Mass.
Tilton School	Tilton, N.H.
Vermont Academy	Saxton's River, Vt.
The Ethel Walker School	Simsbury, Conn.
Walnut Hill	Natick, Mass.
Emma Willard School	Troy, N.Y.
Williston-Northampton School	Easthampton, Mass.
The Winchendon Academy	Winchendon, Mass.
Worcester Academy	Worcester, Mass.

[a]Now The Loomis-Chaffee School.

[b]Now the Northfield-Mount Hermon School.

152

Day Schools

Name	Location
The Blake School	Hopkins, Minn.
Hawken School	Gates Mills, Ohio
The Lakeside School	Seattle, Wash.
The Latin School of Chicago	Chicago, Ill.
Polytechnic School	Pasadena, Calif.
Rye Country Day Schools	Rye, N.Y.
The Westminister School	Atlanta, Ga.

References

Albert, E.M., and Kluckholm, C.K.M. *A selected bibliography on values, ethics, and esthetics in the behavioral sciences and philosophy, 1920-1958.* Glencoe, Ill.: The Free Press, 1960.

Aries, P. *Centuries of childhood.* London: Jonathan Cope, 1962.

Auchincloss, L. *The rector of Justin.* New York: Random House, 1965.

Baird, L.L. Factors in the continuance of accomplishment from high school to college. *Measurement and Evaluation in Guidance,* 1969a, 2, 5-18.

Baird, L.L. Prediction of accomplishment in college: A study of achievement. *Journal of Counseling Psychology,* 1969b, *16,* 246-253.

Baird, L.L. Big school, small school: A critical examination of the hypothesis. *Journal of Educational Psychology,* 1969c, *60,* 253-260.

Baird, L.L. Patterns of educational aspiration. *ACT Research Report No. 32.* Iowa City, Iowa, American College Testing Program, 1970.

Baird, L.L. *Using self-reports to predict student performance.* Monograph No. 7. New York: College Entrance Examination Board, 1976.

Baird, L.L.; Clark, M.J.; and Hartnett, R.T. *The graduates.* Princeton, N.J.: Educational Testing Service, 1973.

Barron, F.X. *Creativity and personal freedom.* Princeton, N.J.: Van Nostrand, 1968.

Barry, R., and Wolf, B. *Motives, values and realities.* New York: Teachers College Press, 1967.

Bayer, A.E., and Boruch, R.I. The black student in American colleges. *ACE Research Report,* Vol. 4, No. 2, 1969.

Berdie, R.F.; Pilapil, B.; and Im, J.I. Entrance correlates of university satisfaction. *American Educational Research Journal,* 1970, 7, 251-266.

Berelson, B., and Steiner, G.A. *Human behavior: An inventory of scientific findings.* New York: Harcourt, Brace and World, 1964.

Blackmer, A.R. *An inquiry into student unrest in independent secondary schools.* Boston: National Association of Independent Schools, 1970.

Bragdon, H.D. *Counseling the college student* (original, 1929). New York: Johnson Reprints, 1965.

Bronfenbrenner, U. *Two worlds of childhood.* New York: Free Press, 1970.

Buhler, C., and Massarik, F. (eds.). *The course of human life: A study of goals in the humanistic perspective.* New York: Springer, 1968.

Centers, R. *The psychology of social classes.* Russell Sage Foundation, 1961.

Clark, B.R. *Educating the expert society.* San Francisco: Chandler, 1962.

Clark, B.R., and Trow, M. The organizational context. *In* T.M. Newcomb, and E.K. Wilson (eds.), *College Peer Groups.* Aldine, 1966.

Coleman, J.S., et al. *Equality of educational opportunity.* Washington, D.C.: U.S. Department of Health, Education, and Welfare, USOE, 1966.

Cox, C. The early mental traits of 300 geniuses. *Genetic studies of genius. Vol. II.* Stanford: Stanford University Press, 1926.

Dornhoff, G.W. *Who rules America?* Englewood Cliffs, N.J.: Prentice-Hall, 1967.

Eiduson, B.L. *Scientists, their psychological world.* New York: Basic Books, 1962.

Elkin, F.E., and Westley, W.A. The myth of adolescent culture. *American Sociological Review*, 1955, *20*, 680-684.

Esty, J.C. *Choosing a private school.* New York: Dodd, Mead, 1974.

Eurich, A.C. Managing the future: Some practical suggestions. *In* J. Caffrey, (ed.), *The future academic community.* Washington: American Council on Education, 1969.

Feldman, K.A., and Newcomb, T.M. *The impact of college on students.* San Francisco: Jossey-Bass, 1969.

Fichter, J.H. *Jesuit high schools revisited.* Washington: Jesuit Educational Association, 1969.

Gaines, R.L. *The finest education money can buy: A concerned look at America's prestige schools.* New York: Simon and Schuster, 1972.

Gross, E., and Grambsch, P.V. *University goals and academic power.* Washington, D.C.: American Council on Education, 1968.

Guskin, A.E., and Guskin, S.L. *A social psychology of education.* Reading, Mass.: Addison-Wesley, 1970.

The handbook of private schools. Boston: Porter-Sargent, 1976.

Henderson, A.G. Control in higher education: Trends and issues. *Journal of Higher Education*, 1969, *40*, 13-26.

Henry, J. *Culture against man.* New York: Random House, 1963.

Holland, J.L., and Richards, J.M., Jr. Academic and non-academic accomplishments: Correlated or uncorrelated? *Journal of Educational Psychology*, 1965, *56*, 165-174.

Hoyt, D.P. College grades and adult accomplishment: A review of research. *Educational Record*, 1966, *47*, 70-75.

Jencks, C.; Smith, M.; Ackland, H.; Bane, M.J.; Cohen, D.; Gintis, H.; Heyns, B.; and Michelson, S. *Inequality: A reassessment of the effect of family and schooling in America.* New York: Basic Books, 1972.

Kohlberg, L. Moral development and the education of adolescents. *In* R. Purnell (ed.). *Adolescents and the American high school.* New York: Holt, Rinehart, and Winston, 1970, pp. 144-62.

Kraushaar, O.F. *American nonpublic schools: Patterns of diversity.* Baltimore: The Johns Hopkins University Press, 1972.

Lane, W.C. The lower class girl in college: A study of Stanford freshman women. Ph.D. dissertation, Stanford University, 1960.

MacKinnon, D.W. The nature and nurture of creative talent. *American Psychologist*, 1962, 484-495.

Mallery, D. *Negro students in independent schools.* Boston: National Association of Independent Schools, 1963.

Mallery, D. *Independence and community in our schools.* Boston: National Association of Independent Schools, 1971.

Matthews, D.R. *U.S. senators and their world.* New York: Vintage, 1960.

Matza, D. Position and behavior patterns of youth. *In* R.E.L. Faris (ed.), *Handbook of modern sociology.* Chicago: Rand-McNally, 1964.

McLachlan, J. *American boarding schools: A historical study.* New York: Scribner's, 1970.

Mills, C.W. *The power elite.* New York: Oxford University Press, Galaxy Books, 1959.

Muuss, R.E. *Theories of adolescence.* New York: Random House, 1966.

Newcomb, T.M. *The acquaintance process.* New York: Holt, 1961.

Nichols, R.C., and Holland, J.L. Prediction of the first year college performance of high aptitude students. *Psychological Monographs,* 1963, 77 (Whole No. 570).

Nichols, R.C., and Holland, J.L. The selection of high aptitude high school graduates for maximum achievement in college. *Personnel and Guidance Journal,* 1964, *43*, 33-40.

Pace, C.R. *The use of CUES in the college admissions process.* College Entrance Examination Board Report No. 2. Los Angeles: University of California, 1966.

Peterson, R.E. *The crisis of purpose: Definition and uses of institutional goals.* Washington, D.C.: ERIC Clearinghouse of Higher Education, 1970.

Prescott, P.S. *A world of our own: Notes on life and learning in a boy's preparatory school.* New York: Coward-McCann, 1970.

Reich, C.A. *The greening of America.* New York: Bantam, 1971.

Remmers, H.H., and Radler, D.H. *The American teenager.* Indianapolis: Bobbs-Merrill, 1957.

Revel, J.F. *Without Marx or Jesus.* New York: Dell, 1974.

Richards, J.M., Jr., and Holland, J.L. A factor analysis of student "explanations" of their choice of a college. *ACT Research Reports, No. 8.* Iowa City, Iowa: American College Testing Program, 1965.

Richards, J.M., Jr.; Holland, J.L.; and Lutz, S.W. The prediction of student accomplishment in college. *Journal of Educational Psychology,* 1967, *58*, 343-355.

Rieff, P. *Freud: The mind of a moralist.* New York: Viking Press, 1959.

Roe, A. *The making of a scientist.* New York: Dodd, Mead & Company, 1953.

Sarason, S.B. *The culture of the school and the problem of change.* New York: Allyn and Bacon, Inc., 1971.

Secondary School Admissions Test Board. *Independent secondary schools: A handbook.* Princeton, N.J.: Educational Testing Service, 1971, 1975, 1976.

Smith, M.B. Personal values in the study of lives. *In* R.W. White (ed.), *The study of lives.* New York: Atherton Press, 1963.

Spady, W.G. Status, achievement, and motivation in the American high school. *School Review,* 1971, *79*, 379-404.

Strommen, M.P.; Brekke, M.L.; Underwager, R.C.; and Johnson, A.L. *A study of generations.* Minneapolis: Ausburg Publishing House, 1972.

Taylor, C.W., and Ellison, R.L. Biographical predictors of scientific performance. *Science*, 1967, *155*, 1075-1080.

Taylor, C.W., and Holland, J.L. Predictors of creative performance. *In* C.W. Taylor (ed.), *Creativity: Progress and potential.* New York: McGraw-Hill, 1964.

Turner, R.H. *The social context of ambition.* San Francisco: Chandler Publishing Company, 1964.

Tyler, L.E. *The work of the counselor* (2nd Ed.). New York: Appleton-Century-Crofts, 1961.

Volsky, T., Jr.; Maggon, R.M.; Norman, W.T.; and Hoyt, D.P. *The outcomes of counseling and psychotherapy.* Minneapolis: University of Minnesota Press, 1965.

Warren, J.R. *College grading practices, an overview.* Washington, D.C.: ERIC Clearinghouse of Higher Education, 1971.

Yankelovich, D. *The new morality: A profile of American youth in the 70's.* New York: McGraw-Hill, 1974.

Index

Index

Creativity, 143-145
Curriculum of schools, 2, 136, 144
Cushing Academy, 1, 151

Dalton, Edward, xi
Dana Hall School, 151
Day schools, tuition, 2
Deerfield Academy, 5, 151
Developmental tasks, students progress
    on, 115-119
Dobbs (Master's School), 151
Dornhoff, G. William, xiii, 154
Dummer School (Governor Dummer
    Academy), 151

Effects of schools on students, 107-
    121
Eiduson, B.L., 61, 144, 154
Elitism of schools, charges of, xiii
Elkin, F.E., 24, 154
Emma Willard School, 5
Esty, J.C., 133, 154
Ethel Walker School, 3
Eurich, Alvin, 97, 154
Exeter, Phillips Academy, 11, 12
Expectation of students for schools,
    18-19
Experimental programs, xiv, 3, 4
Extracurricular activities, 60-64
    importance for students' develop-
        ment, 61-62, 145
    influence on students' status, 24-26
    and popularity with opposite sex,
        31-33
    satisfaction with, 62-64

Faculty. See Teachers
Feldman, Kenneth A., 41, 59, 154
Fichter, Joseph, 88, 154
Future of the elite schools, 104-106,
    141-146

Gaines, Richard L., 78-79, 84, 143,
    154
Girls' schools. See Single sex schools
Goals of schools. See Purposes
Governing board members, relations
    of, with school, 72-73, 74

Grading practices in the schools, 57-59
Grambsch, P.V., 97
Gross, E., 97, 154
Groton, 6, 10, 151
Guskin, A.E., 154
Guskin, S.L., 154

Hawken School, 152
Headmasters. See Heads of schools
Heads of schools
    administrative functions of, 73-74
    changing expectations of, 50
    complex job of, 50, 74
    as keys to schools' effectiveness, 74
    power of, 72-73
    as seen by teachers and trustees, 74
Hebron Academy, 7, 46, 61, 151
Helms, Marian, xi
Henderson, A.G., 96, 154
Henry, J., 88, 154
Hill School, 2, 151
Holland, John, 143, 144, 154
Holt, John, 56, 57
Hotchkiss School, 151
Hoyt, Donald P., 143, 144, 154
Hutchins, Robert, 49

Ibsen, Henrick, 132
Identity, student, 111-112
Impact of schools on students, 112-
    115, 116-121, 130-134
    limitations of, 119-121
Independent schools. See also Stu-
    dents; Teachers; other specific
    topics
    age, 1
    black students in, 36-42
    comparisons with public schools,
        123-134
    curricula, 2, 3
    diversity of, 1-8
    effects on students, 107-121
    endowment funds of, 2
    facilities of, 4, 5, 141
    impact on student, 112-115, 116-
        121
    location, 7
    philosophy, 96-104, 127, 128

About the Author

Leonard L. Baird received the Ph.D. from the University of California, Los Angeles. He is now a senior research psychologist at the Educational Testing Service in Princeton, New Jersey. He has written over fifty articles and several monographs on educational environments, predicting academic success, testing, and the entrance of students into colleges and graduate and professional schools.